VOICE AND
THE ACTOR

VOICE AND THE ACTOR

by

CICELY BERRY

HARRAP LONDON

First published in Great Britain 1973
by GEORGE G. HARRAP & CO. LTD
182-184 High Holborn, London WC1V 7AX

Reprinted: 1974; 1976

© Cicely Berry 1973

ISBN 0 245 52012 0 (boards)
ISBN 0 245 52021 X (limp)

Printed in Great Britain by
Redwood Burn Limited, Trowbridge & Esher

Foreword by Peter Brook

Exercises are very much in fashion in the theatre: in fact, for some groups they have become a way of life. Yet we have a healthy instinct that rebels against the thought of exercises: in some parts of the world, people still sing for the joy of singing, dance for the joy of dancing, doing neither physical nor vocal training, while their muscles and vocal cords unerringly perform whatever is expected of them. Are exercises then really necessary? Would it not be enough to trust nature and act by instinct?

Cicely Berry has based her work on the conviction that while all is present in nature our natural instincts have been crippled from birth by many processes — by the conditioning, in fact, of a warped society. So an actor needs precise exercise and clear understanding to liberate his hidden possibilities and to learn the hard task of being true to 'the instinct of the moment'.

As her book points out with remarkable persuasiveness 'technique' as such is a myth, for there is no such thing as a correct voice. There is no right way — there are only a million wrong ways, which are wrong because they deny what would otherwise be affirmed. Wrong uses of the voice are those that constipate feeling, constrict activity, blunt expression, level out idiosyncrasy, generalize experience, coarsen intimacy. These blockages are multiple and are the results of acquired habits that have become part of the automatic vocal equipment; unnoticed and unknown, they stand between the actor's voice as it is and as it could be and they will not vanish by themselves.

So the work is not how to do but how to permit: how, in fact, to set the voice free. And since life in the voice springs from emotion, drab and uninspiring technical exercises can never be sufficient. Cicely Berry never departs from the fundamental recognition that speaking is part of a whole: an expression of inner life. She insists on poetry because good verse strikes echoes in the speaker that awaken portions of his deep experience which are seldom evoked in everyday speech. After a voice session with her I have known actors speak not of the voice but of a growth in human relationships. This is a high tribute to work that is the opposite of specialization. Cicely Berry sees the voice teacher as involved in all of a theatre's work. She would never try to separate the sound of words from their living context. For her the two are inseparable.

This is what makes her book so necessary and valuable.

ACKNOWLEDGMENTS

We would like to thank the following for their kind permission to print the poems and extracts included in this book:

The Trustees of the Hardy Estate, The Macmillan Company of Canada and Macmillan, London and Basingstoke (Copyright 1925 by Macmillan Publishing Co., Inc.), for 'The Going' from *Collected Poems*, by Thomas Hardy; the Estate of the late Mrs Frieda Lawrence and Laurence Pollinger Ltd, for 'Tortoise Shout' from *The Complete Poems of D.H. Lawrence* ed. by Vivian de Sola Pinto and F. Warren Roberts, © 1964, 1971 by Angelo Ravagli and C.M. Weekley, Executors of the Estate of Frieda Lawrence Ravagli. Reprinted by permission of the Viking Press, Inc.; The Society of Authors, on behalf of the Bernard Shaw Estate, for an extract from *Man and Superman*; Edith Sitwell and Macmillan, London and Basingstoke, for 'Scotch Rhapsody' from *Collected Poems*; J.M. Dent & Sons Ltd, the Trustees for the copyrights of the late Dylan Thomas and the New Directions Publishing Corporation, for an extract from *Under Milk Wood* and 'Over Sir John's Hill' from *Collected Poems*, by Dylan Thomas; the Macmillan Company of London and Basingstoke and the Macmillan Company of Canada Ltd, for 'Easter 1916' from *The Collected Poems of W.B. Yeats*, © 1924 by Macmillan Publishing Co., Inc., renewed 1952 by Bertha Georgie Yeats. Reprinted with permission of Macmillan.

We would also like to thank Philip Sayer, photographer, and Lynn Dearth, actress, for the photographs.

Contents

	Page
Introduction	7
1 Vocal Development	11
2 Relaxation and Breathing	18
3 Muscularity and Word	43
4 The Whole Voice	76
5 Speaking Poetry	101
6 Listening	123
7 Using the Voice	130
Summary of Exercises	137

ILLUSTRATIONS

DIAGRAMS IN TEXT · *Page*

Resonating spaces	10
Possible rib movement	21
Good and bad positions on the floor	23
Bone-prop in the mouth	49
Position of tongue and its movement	53
Palate lowered	55
Position of back of tongue and soft palate	56

PHOTOGRAPHS · *Plate*

Incorrect posture	1
Correct posture	2
Free position on the floor	3
Tense position of neck and shoulders	4
Good breathing position	5
Demonstrating rib movement	6
Hands stretched above the head	7
Hands and head hung down	8

Introduction

The voice is the means by which, in everyday life, you communicate
with other people, and though, of course, how you present yourself —
your posture, movement, dress and involuntary gesture — gives an
impression of your personality, it is through the speaking voice that
you convey your precise thoughts and feelings. This also involves the
amount of vocabulary you have at your disposal and the particular
words you choose. It follows, therefore, that the more responsive and
efficient the voice is, the more accurate it will be to your intentions.

The voice is the most intricate mixture of what you hear, how you
hear it, and how you unconsciously choose to use it in the light of
your personality and experience. This is complex, as you will see, and
is conditioned by four factors:

Environment. As children you learn to speak unconsciously,
because of your needs and because you are influenced by the sounds
you hear spoken around you. It is an imitative process, so that you
start to talk roughly in the same way as the family, or the unit in
which you grow up — that is, with a similar tune and with similar
vowels and consonants. Possibly the facility with which you convey
your needs, and the resistance to or compliance with them at this
very early stage, influences the individual use of pitch later — how
easily you get what you want, in fact.

'Ear'. By this I mean the perception of sound. Some people hear
sounds more distinctly than others, and some people are more
accurate in their production of them. If you have a good 'ear' you
are open to a greater number of different notes in the voice and to
the differing shades of vowels and consonants. This is involved with
pleasure in sound and you are aware of a larger spectrum of choice
than that provided by your immediate environment. Perhaps you are
quicker to see what the voice can do for you.

Physical agility. People have varying degrees of muscular awareness
and freedom; this is partly due to environment, though not completely,
for it is also tied up with the ease with which you feel you can express
yourself in speech, and this of course is to some extent conditioned
by education. An introverted and thoughtful person often finds more
difficulty in speaking, and does not carry the thought through into
the physical process of making speech. There is a kind of reluctance
in committing oneself to speech, and this certainly affects the muscles
involved in making speech, making their movement less firm and so
the result less positive. The less you wish to communicate in speech,
the less firmly you use the muscles, and this of course has much to do

7

with confidence. It very rarely has anything to do with laziness. Furthermore, some people think more quickly than they speak, so they trip over words and the result is unfinished. You have to relate the mental intention to the physical action.

Personality. It is in the light of your own self that you interpret the last three conditions, by which you unconsciously form your own voice. So that, though you start by imitation, it is your emotional reaction to your family and environment, your degree of sensitivity to sound, your own individual need to communicate, and your ease or unease in doing so, which are the contributory factors that make you evolve your own completely personal voice and speech.

The voice, therefore, is incredibly sensitive to what is going on around it. In very broad terms, the speech of people who live in country districts is usually slower and more musical than the speech evolved in cities, which is nearly always sharp and glottal and quick − for example, New York, London and Glasgow have very similar speech characteristics. The condition of life conditions the speech, so that the rhythm, pitch and inflection vary accordingly. In the same way, but to an infinitely more subtle degree, personal relationships and the degree of ease with one's environment and situation continually affect the individual's voice.

Now the image you have of your own voice is often disturbingly different from the way it actually sounds to other people. It often does not tally with how you think of yourself. Most people are shocked, for instance, when they hear their voice recorded for the first time − it sounds affected, high-pitched, sloppy or just dull. Hearing it recorded is not necessarily a good test, as the mechanism is selective and does not give a whole picture of the voice, just as a photograph, while true, does not give a whole picture of the person. However, you do not hear your own voice as other people hear it, partly because you hear it via the bone conduction and vibrations in your own head, so that you never hear the end product. But, more important, you hear it subjectively − that is, tied up with your own conceptions of sound, of how you would like to sound, and also tied up with what you know you want to convey, for you are on the inside. So the impression you have of your own voice is completely subjective. The result is that you can never be quite sure of the impression you are making, or how accurate your voice is to your intentions − it quite often belies them.

Because it is such a personal statement, criticism of your voice is very close to criticism of yourself, and can easily be destructive. What you need to do is open up the possibilities of your voice and find out what it can do, and try to find a balance between being subjective and objective about it.

This you can do by exercising its physical resources, and perhaps by being bolder in the standards you set yourself. Speaking and using the voice is partly a physical action involving the use of certain muscles, and, just as an athlete goes into training to get his muscles to the required efficiency, or a pianist practises to make his fingers more agile, so if you exercise the muscles involved in using the voice, you can increase its efficiency in sound.

Let us see quite simply how sound is made. To make a sound two factors are needed, something that strikes and something that is struck and which resists the impact to a greater or lesser degree and vibrates accordingly. These vibrations disturb the surrounding air and set up sound waves which you receive through the ear and interpret accordingly. If the sound happens in a room the space will amplify the sound; the emptier the space and the less porous the walls, the more it will be amplified. For instance, a stone building such as a church amplifies sound relatively more than a room which may have materials in it which absorb sound, and where the walls are more porous. Now, a musical sound has a third factor which is a resonant, either a resonating space or resonating material, such as wood, which amplifies the initial sound and sustains it so you hear a note of resultant pitch. Take, for example, a violin: the bow strikes the strings which vibrate according to their length and tautness, these vibrations disturb the surrounding air and set up sound waves which your ear then transmits into sound, and you hear a violin note. The initial sound, however, is amplified and resonated by the wooden case of the violin, and that wooden box sets up its own vibrations which are the harmonics of the original note and which give that note the particular quality of the violin. The sound of one violin can also vary enormously from the sound of another. The quality of the bow and strings, the precise measurements of the box and the quality of its wood, how it is made, and so on, make the resonating vibrations different and so set up slightly different harmonics. Thus, the sound from two different instruments is still recognizable as a note from a violin, though the quality of the note can vary enormously. Furthermore, the way in which the player uses the instrument can make an enormous difference to the sound. The length and tautness of the strings determines the pitch.

You can make an analogy between the violin and the voice. With the voice the breath is the initial impulse, which strikes against the vocal cords in the larynx, which have come together, and makes them vibrate. This sets up sound waves which can then be resonated in the chest, the pharynx or hollow space above the larynx, in the mouth and nose and bones of the face, and the hollow spaces in the head (the sinuses).

Physically, one person varies in size and shape from another person, so each individual voice is intrinsically different. But it is how you

9

use the breath, how you use the resonating spaces, that matters, and it is important, therefore, that you use them as well as possible.

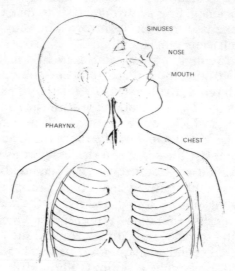

1 Vocal Development

The most useful part of this book will certainly be the exercises, for it is the exercises that matter. It is by doing them, and doing them regularly, that you will increase the physical awareness of your voice and give yourself the freedom to experience the resonances of which you are capable.

The exercises laid out at the back are a synthesis of those in the main part of the book and, as by the end I hope you will have experienced a new awareness of your voice, they will act as a guide and reminder of what you will have found to be necessary and useful to you.

But it is important that you do not look on exercises only as a reassurance of physical prowess. They are a preparation, both physical and for your whole self, which will enable you to respond instinctively to any situation. It is only if, as an actor, you are in a state of total readiness that you are free to be part of the action, which is new every moment. In other words, you do not have to come out of the situation to reflect and think 'How can I do this?'; you do it at the moment the action arises, because the voice is so free. Exercises should not make you more technical, but more free.

You will also find that doing exercises leads you to know something more of yourself and your attitude towards acting.

It seems to me that the development of the voice goes through three stages. You do exercises for relaxation, breathing and for the increased muscularity of the lips and tongue, all of which free you and open up the voice almost as you do them. You find more power with less effort, more incisiveness, and you hear notes in the voice that you did not know you had, and which are surprising. This is the first stage, and an encouraging one. It is important because it gives proof of the potential sound you have. You can hear the benefit of the exercises on texts which you use to stretch the voice and make it more responsive.

When you come to the second stage, that of applying this freedom and flexibility to the work which you are presenting to an audience, then the business becomes more complex. You will very likely find that the vocal tensions and limitations you normally have are an integral part of the tensions and limitations you have in communicating as an actor, and are therefore not easy to discard. You are therefore forced to question and adjust your whole acting process, for you cannot consider voice by itself, only in relation to the job you are doing.

For example, some actors have an overbalance of head resonance.

11

This comes from tension in the back of the palate and tongue which does not allow the chest notes to reinforce the sound. It also comes, I think, from a mistaken idea that that is where the sound should be placed. This concentration of energy in the head resonators gives the voice a metallic quality which carries well, the actor hears it in his head as having bite and edge, qualities on which he feels he can rely, and his ear is accustomed to that sound. In fact, to the listener's ear the texture of the voice is restricted, because it is thin and lacks the warmth that the chest notes could give it — its wholeness — and so its possibilities are narrowed. By taking this particular tension away, rooting the voice down, and finding the energy in a different place with less conscious effort, the voice will have much greater flexibility and freedom; it will also have more conviction because it will be more complete. All this the actor may feel when doing the exercises on his own, but when faced with the situation of the audience it is extremely difficult for him to believe that he is being as positive when he is not feeling the usual effort. He feels lost without the tension on which he has relied, because this tension was part of his emotional make-up and his way of committing himself to an audience, and perhaps of convincing himself. It then becomes more than a simple question of voice, for the rooted voice is stronger and more positive — it calls into question your judgment of the amount of energy needed to communicate, and where that energy should be found. Whatever the problem, it takes time to believe that freedom works.

It is obviously difficult to talk about voice in general terms, because the voice is absolutely personal to the individual. It is the means by which you communicate your inner self, and there are many factors, both physical and psychological, which have contributed to its making, so that the danger is that you will interpret instructions subjectively. You therefore have to discover a very firm basis of understanding, a common understanding, a norm, and this you can do by the experience of exercises and the precise movements of muscles, and their effect on the voice.

Tensions and limitations always come from a lack of trust in yourself: either you are over-anxious to communicate or to present an image, or you want to convince an audience of something about yourself. Even the experienced actor often limits himself by relying too much on what he knows works and is effective, and this in itself is a lack of freedom. Certainly, an actor has to find what means he can rely on to communicate to his audience, that is part of the craft, but if he holds on to the same means to find his energy and truth he then becomes predictable. He fixes, and what started as something which was good can end so easily as a manner — the same way of dealing with a situation. An actor with an interesting voice who uses it well can still end up with his audience knowing how he is going to sound, so there is no surprise. This has a lot to do with lack of trust, because it takes trust to start each part with a clean slate, as it were — in other words, with no preconceived ideas of how it should sound, no holding on to the voice that you know. It is only by being in a state of readiness that the voice will be liberated.

This second stage, therefore, often involves discarding what is comfortable. It involves persevering with the exercises so that we learn about energy — where our energy lies and how to use it. All unnecessary tension is wasted energy. More than this, if you do not use enough energy you fail to reach your audience, but if you use too much you disperse it by using too much breath, bursting out on consonants, by being too loud, and so on. The audience then tends to recoil, because you are pushing the energy, manufacturing it, and not finding it within yourself, and this has to do with pushing out emotion and underlining what you feel. In real life you step back from the person who is over-anxious, over-enthusiastic, the person who gets you in a corner when he talks to you, and it is the same with the actor's relationship with his audience. What you are attempting to find is the right physical balance in the voice, which of course helps the acting balance — the more often you find it, the easier it is to recall it. It is in persevering with the voice over a period of time that you get the essential awareness of the separateness of muscles and what they contribute, and this is when voice finds its own intrinsic quality, involving no effort. It is a two-way process, and a rather marvellous one, you know what you want to communicate, but in the physical act of making sound, meanings take on a new dimension.

In short, you are looking for the energy in the muscles them-selves, and when you find that energy you do not have to push it out, it releases itself. You do not then have to push your emotion out, it is released through the voice. When you can tie this up with your intentions as an actor you have found what you are after, a unity of physical and emotional energy, and you are then at the third stage. Here the aim is only to simplify. Quite suddenly the very simple exercises take on a particular purpose, and you are round again to the view that the straightforward exercises for relaxation, breathing and the muscularity of the lips and tongue are your basis and your security.

So, though in the end getting the best out of your voice is a straight matter of doing exercises, you often have to go through a complex phase to know why the exercises are needed. Because you cannot divorce voice from communication, you have to sort out the problems and needs of communication before the exercises can be effective. And communication to an audience is complex and elusive,

13

its validity changes as you change and with the different material you are using. The aim is always clarity, but you can fog that clarity by allowing too much feeling through, by over-explaining, by presenting what you think you ought to present, what you think is interesting, that is to say, by selecting the part of yourself which you think is most acceptable. And you can fog it by tension, which is always a matter of compensating for something you think you lack — size, for instance. A slightly-built actor will very often push his voice down in a false way in an effort to get weight, but this only limits and diminishes, and he has to learn to trust in his own size. You continually signal what you would like people to see of you, and when you signal that you feel, that you understand, then you fog real communication.

I think one of the greatest fears of the actor is that of not being interesting. This really need never be a fear because everyone is interesting in that he is himself. When you get to the point which says 'This is me; it will change, and perhaps improve, but this is me at this moment', then the voice will become open. Certainly, the more integrated the actor is the more he realizes the value of specific exercises. That is why I said that our common ground was the experience of the voice through the movement of muscles, and each person has to apply this experience for himself. The more you do this, the more objective you will become.

The primary object then is to open up the possibilities of the voice, and to do this you have to start listening. I do not mean listening to the external sound of your voice; I mean very specially listening *for* the vocal resource you have, listening *for* what you as a person require to say, and listening *for* what the text contains. And this takes time and stillness. You are conditioned so much by what you think good sound should be, by what you would like the result to be, which is often too logical anyway, that you limit the range of notes you use and stop your instinctive responses. You get ready with your sound before you have really listened to what is being said to you, or before you have really listened to what your text says. This again is a form of anxiety which makes you rush into things. You have to learn to listen afresh in every moment, and to keep questioning what you are saying; only by doing this can you keep the voice truly alive.

A great deal of voice work is done on what, to my mind, is a negative basis — this is, 'correcting' the voice, making it 'better', with all the social and personal implications of that word, somehow making it seem that you are not quite good enough. Emphasis has been on ironing out not-quite-standard vowels, neatening consonants, projecting the voice, and getting a full, consistent tone, with the underlying inference that there is a way that you should sound, a way of

14

speaking lines. Naturally, the voice must be able to give pleasure, and it can only do so if it is well tuned and rhythmically aware, and this involves well-defined vowels and consonants. Additionally, however, you must always build on the vitality which is there in your own voice, increase your awareness of its music so that it can fulfil the demands of a text, and make the vowels and consonants more accurate because that way you are alive to the accuracy of the meaning. A corrective attitude to voice reduces the actor to using it 'right', and keeps him within the conventional tramlines of good speech. This way it cannot be accurate to himself. It is also inhibiting, and makes much acting dull. You want to open the voice out so that its music can match the music of what you are saying, and make the vowels and consonants sharp so you can point the meaning.

I think many young, interesting actors shy away from working on voice because of this restrictive attitude. Quite understandably they do not want something so personal interfered with and sounding well produced; they distrust it for they fear their individuality will be lost, and in any case it is not relevant to what they feel. This kind of attitude is a relic of all the associations of class which attached to English speech, thankfully now becoming less significant. If you have any sort of regional accent or slightly 'off-gent' speech, subconsciously there is the fear that if you make it standard you will lose some of your vitality, and consequently some of your virility, and this is a very real barrier. It may also seem as though you are betraying your background. Nevertheless, if you hold on to a way of speaking for the wrong reason you limit your voice, and therefore you limit what it can convey. If you limit it consciously, then the voice will not be quite true, and it follows that the acting will not be quite right. It is as crucial as that. Limitations keep the audience attention on the actor and not on the character he is playing.

As you can see, it is a delicate balance to keep the essential truth of your own voice, yet make it large and malleable enough to use it for feelings which are other than your own and which have to be projected, whether to a large auditorium, as in the theatre, or in a smaller way for a TV or film camera. To get this balance you have to work in two ways, technically and imaginatively, the one reaffirming the other. Therefore you have to use all the methods at your disposal, even if they sometimes seem contradictory, because you are working from two ends — but you will meet in the middle.

Singing, of course, is an excellent way to stretch the voice. It strengthens the breathing and makes you find and use resonances in the chest and head. Most importantly, I think, it gives you a useful experience of feeling sound bouncing off, an effortlessness in which the emotions are not involved too much. Useful because you so often push emotions too much, and you need the experience of being

15

able to allow the voice to come out freely. However, the actor must never think of his voice as an instrument, as this implies something exterior to himself with which he can do things, and then it will be false. Naturally, it needs to sound interesting, but interesting and remarkable in so far as what you are saying is interesting and remarkable and not as an end in itself. Again it is a balance you are dealing with, of having feeling but at the same time being able to let go of it. I think it is important to recognize the difference between training the voice for singing and training it for acting, because many misconceptions can arise about where sound should be placed. For both you need to open up everything you have, but for singing you convey your meanings through the particular disciplines of sound — the sound is the message — so that the energy is in the resonance. For the actor, on the other hand, the voice is an extension of himself and the possibilities are as complex as the actor himself, and so it means a basic difference in the balance of sound and word. For the actor, ultimately it is the word that must impinge, as it is the word which contains the result of his feeling and his thought; it is therefore in the word that his energy must lie, and in the million ways of stressing, lengthening and inflecting it. This is why an overbalance of head tone does not communicate to an audience — it does not reinforce the word.

Your voice must be accurate to yourself, so it needs to reflect not only what you think and feel but also your physical presence. Because you are dealing with words that are not your own, that come off a printed page, you have to be continually finding ways to make them your own. Obviously, all the work you do in searching for the intellectual and emotional motive will inform the words and make the speech alive, but you can further this process by becoming as sensitive as possible to the physical make-up of your voice in relation to your body. As you open the breathing out in the base of the ribs and the diaphragm and stomach, so you are able to feel where the sound starts, and you can root it down, as it were, so that the whole frame of the body is involved with and is part of the sound. This is its physical presence. Doing strenuous and free move-ment with voice exercises can give quite extraordinary results, as it takes the concentration into a different area, helps to relate the voice to the body as a whole, and gives you experience of quite different vocal textures. An actor can be working subtly with a lot going on in his mind and imagination, but unless the voice is rooted down it will make no complete statement, and to some degree will negate what is interesting.

Just as breathing is a vital function, so the need to make sound to convey our needs is vital. Words came about because of the physical needs to express a situation. Think for a moment of expressions like 'my heart came into my mouth', 'my hair stood on end' or 'my hackles rose' — these are atavistic phrases which tell you something of your response to fear and of being attacked. You have these sensations when you are frightened and certain anatomical changes take place. You have physiological reactions to all emotions and states of being. Your skin and hair, for instance, behave quite differently when you are feeling good to when you are unhappy or tired.

The words are rooted with the breath. I do not believe this can be achieved by a lot of patter exercises because they are meaningless and do not in any way contribute to your awareness of the physical root of words or their possibilities. It always seems to me a waste of time to work on any text that is second-rate; the better the text the more possibilities will open up.

It is difficult to do voice exercises on your own, partly because of the indecision of what to do, and also because of the discouraging feeling that you may be doing them wrong. Just the responsibility of doing them makes for tension. However, if the exercises are set out it is not so difficult to follow instructions, and I think those appearing in this book are foolproof. Obviously you will not be able to go through all of them each time, but I shall work through the exercises in the next two chapters because it is important that you understand the progression that is there. For example, the relaxation and breathing on the floor takes a good deal more time than when sitting or standing, because it takes time to feel the openness, so it may not be possible to do these particular exercises every time you practise, but if you understand the principle it helps through the other exercises. It is much better to do half an hour a day, and stick to that period, than feel you have to do an hour and then not do it because you are unable to find the time.

Everyone is at different stages and has varying needs, yet all basically require to do something from each section, for the exercises are interrelated. As the exercises become easier so the process becomes quicker and you can be more selective as to what to do to achieve your result.

As you will see, the exercises operate at different levels. At times you need to use them purely as exercise to make you ready for work. At other times you are conscious of them tying up with deeper problems which they help to solve. In any case the act of doing them is always productive.

2 Relaxation and Breathing

What you require is as open and full a tone as possible, yet one which is completely your own. You want to increase range and power, and to be able to call on it as you need.

The voice is incredibly sensitive to any feelings of unease. In everyday life, if you are slightly nervous or not quite on top of the situation, this condition reacts on the voice. The basic feeling of fear puts all the defence mechanisms into action, and the result is tension, particularly in the upper part of the body, the neck and shoulders.

The actor knows just how dependent he is on his voice, and what demands he wants to make on it, and this knowledge in itself makes for tension. The great problem is the ever-varying one of space. If he has to fill a large space it must be without seeming effort, without coarsening his voice or cutting down on the intimacy of tone; in a film or TV studio, however, he has to use his voice with a high degree of naturalism, yet keep its particular edge, meaning and colour (which is not at all like talking naturally).

Size is therefore the first thing I shall deal with, as it is possibly the biggest cause of tension. At the moment I do not mean the size of a character — emotional size — as we shall talk about that later. Here I mean simply the size needed to fill a theatre. It is only partly to do with volume; it is also partly an attitude — a reaching out of oneself to an audience which involves taking your time — and partly the firmness of sound, its solidity which will carry. The important thing is that an audience is only interested in actors talking to each other. As soon as an actor starts talking at another actor or at the audience, the thought ceases to be specific and he loses contact with the audience. They do not want to know. They hear but do not understand.

If you start to push, because of tension, these things are likely to happen:
1 The voice goes up slightly in pitch and takes on a curious, unfocused quality. This irons out the flexibility of the voice, the natural talking inflections, so that we get a rhetorical tone and not a talking or conversational one. The meaning then stops being specific.
2 The sound comes out at the same pressure, which alienates the listener because his ear is being assaulted and not drawn in to listen.
3 The tension in the neck restricts the throat and cuts out the lower tones of the voice, the chest notes. This tension puts, as it were,

a skin on the tone, making it sound the same however much range you may be using. It negates the inflections, so that what you are saying becomes general and not particular.

4 The most important point is that, because the sound is being pushed, the listener is more aware of the sound than of the word.

All this adds up to the same thing; if there is tension in the neck and you try to make your voice big you will push from the throat and so cut out all the interesting undertones of your voice. Your energy is in the wrong place. The throat is the one place that you should feel no effort.

When working in studios the fact that so little volume is needed is inhibiting and misleading. The naturalism you need often makes you use what I call a half-voice, instead of your complete voice at reduced volume, which cuts out a lot of the colour of the voice. Because of the restricted area in which you are working the amount of movement is limited, and any tension you may have is consequently more difficult to break. You cannot get the sense of vocal freedom that is possible on the stage, and the voice is more difficult to manipulate.

The limitations I have mentioned so far may happen in varying degrees; they may happen on some acting parts and not on others, and in some conditions and not in others. The important thing is that tension of any sort cuts down the effectiveness of the actor, and whether or not he is aware of the reason he is aware of being limited. This immediately reacts on his confidence, and he becomes more tense. It can be almost a vicious circle. The old adage about singing best in the bath is quite true. The acoustics of a bathroom are such that they reinforce the resonance of the voice particularly well, so that it sounds good — the result is you actually sing better. This is something one cannot say too much; you have to trust your voice, because it is only then that you will get the best out of it. It blossoms with success, though we must not strive for success too much.

It is obvious that extra force is needed to fill a theatre, and that very particular control is needed in a studio. You have to find where the energy is and how to release it. 'Teach us to care and not to care', as Eliot says. The 'caring' is the work done to prepare, and the 'not caring' is letting it go.

Think again of the analogy of the voice and the violin. The quality of the sound emitted by the violin depends on how the bow is used, the quality of the strings and their tautness, and how well the resonating box is made. With the voice, you depend on the breath to start the sound — not too much for that would make the sound breathy, not too little for that would make the attack glottal and the tone hard, but right and clean and using all the breath to make sound. The vocal cords, which are the strings of the violin, are not under your direct control, so you can do little about them. In fact,

19

you are only aware of them when you misuse them by tension in the larynx, by forcing the sound out before the breath is ready, by being out of time, as it were, constantly using a pitch which is outside your range. You then get nodes or small corns on them, which results in your having no proper control over the sound; this can be a serious condition, best dealt with by a laryngologist.

You depend on the resonating spaces for the quality of sound you produce. Look at the illustration on page 10 to see the possible areas which can vibrate and contribute to the sound.

You can see that there is enormous potential for resonance, or amplification of your primary note. The bones themselves can be part of this amplification, and you can even feel vibration down to the base of the spine and in the stomach. Whether you use this resonance or not depends on the breath and complete freedom, or relaxation — good posture, in fact.

For example, if your back is not as straight as possible the ribs cannot open properly, there is little possibility of movement at the bottom of the rib cage. The curve in the base of the spine results in a hollow back. One curve in the spine automatically makes for another one to compensate and maintain the balance of the body, so the upper part of the chest is pulled back. If you consciously put yourself in this position you will see how impossible it is to open the ribs up round the back, something which is absolutely vital to the solidity of tone and to your own confidence.

Similarly, the base of the back can be in a good position, but if the shoulders are dropped forward the head has to be pulled back, both to compensate for balance and to keep the head in a normal position.

You will find that the resonating space in the neck is completely squashed, so there will be little reinforcement of the tone from there. It is useful to consciously put yourself in these positions in a fairly exaggerated way so that you can feel the results of such tensions. You will also find that one tension leads to another: tension in the small of the back makes you feel tension in the shoulders, for example, while tension in the back of the neck leads to tension in the front of the neck where the larynx or voice-box is, an area where it is particularly bad to have tension because then you can so easily strain the voice. Tensions here lead to tensions in the jaw, and jaw tension has repercussions on the back of the tongue and palate.

Obviously I am overstating these tensions, because it is then easier to understand their effect. Few people have them in such an exaggerated form, yet almost everyone has them to some degree. Tension is likely to come when faced with the necessity of projecting to an audience, and when it does it limits the voice and deprives it of some of its richness and reverberations. The actor's rapport with his audience is then not so happy, for they are aware of his tension and therefore cannot be free to enjoy the illusion which is the aim of every performance.

Just as tension limits the use of the resonating spaces, so it limits the breathing capacity. As I have said, a good note on the violin depends on how the player applies the bow. You depend on breath, and how you apply it.

If you look at the illustration below it is obvious that there is considerable room for movement in the lower part of the chest, where the ribs are attached to the spine at the back, but to each other, by muscle, in the front. In fact, the bottom two pairs are floating — that is, not attached at all in the front. The top six pairs of ribs are firmly attached to the spine at the back and to the sternum, or breastbone, in front. If you breathe from the upper part of the chest, therefore, the whole rib cage has to move and you use a great deal of effort to get a relatively small amount of breath. Unfortunately, a great deal of athletic training concentrates on this area for breath supply as it enables you to take quick, short breaths, and if you have trained in this way it is difficult to break the habit. This type of breathing produces an enormous amount of tension in the upper part of the chest and shoulders which, as we have seen, is totally wrong for the voice.

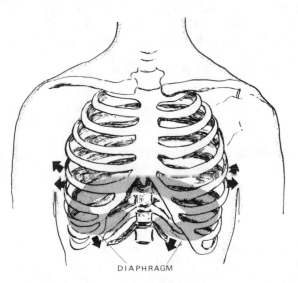

DIAPHRAGM

You obviously need as much breath as possible without effort, and that breath you need to make into sound. If you find the breath at the base of the ribs, especially at the back and in the stomach as the diaphragm descends, then the whole frame of the body becomes part of the sound as it contributes to it with its resonance. You can feel

21

the whole of your spine, right down to its base, being part of the breathing cycle and therefore part of the sound. The result is that the physical presence is in the voice. If your breathing is limited to the upper part of the body your voice will reflect only part of you. You can, in fact, get by with very little breath, manufacturing the vocal energy in the throat, but the result will be what I call 'cerebral' sound – it will reveal nothing beyond what is in your mind and will have no physical or emotional resonances. As I said earlier, physical resonance opens up areas of understanding, of feeling, of emotional resonance, and sometimes just the act of making that sound increases your understanding.

What you are doing is reaching down to your centre for the sound. The breath goes in, and the sound comes out – you are touching down to your centre, you are finding the 'I' of your voice. When you find this it is as though you belong, you are present in what you are saying. You will then find the breath touching off the sound like a drum. You will find that you will not have to use a great deal of breath, because the breath will be made into sound. It is economy of effort. When you find this absolutely right use of breath the voice will be effortless, it will impel itself. This is where your true energy is. This is what I mean by rooting the voice.

You can find this energy quite practically by exercise, but the exercise is useless without the right thought behind it, and vice versa.

It is also clear that relaxation depends on breathing, and breathing on relaxation, which is why you have to do the two types of exercises together.

There are two more things I should like to say before we get down to the exercises. First, about breathing. The process of rooting down takes time, so do not do the exercises quicker than you can feel the whole process working. As soon as you feel the breath touching down you can speed up, as speed comes with efficiency.

The second thing I want to mention is relaxation. It is always difficult to give precise directions about this, because it varies so much with the individual, and you can never be completely sure how the directions will be interpreted. To begin with, I prefer to use the word 'free' to the word 'relaxed', as the latter gives the impression of being floppy and heavy, and therefore perhaps dull, whereas 'free' implies being relaxed but ready for action, alert but not tense. You constantly have to differentiate between the tension you need and the tension you do not need. To make any movement certain muscles have to have tension – just to stand upright involves tension in certain muscles, for example. What you do not want, however, is unnecessary tension, because all unnecessary tension is wasted energy – it is energy being kept in and not made available for communication. This means that you have to be aware of the separate-

22

ness of muscles and what they do, and this is particularly difficult
when you come to work on the neck. Later, when you come to work
on exercises for muscularity in the lips and tongue, you will find how
difficult it is to keep the neck relaxed when increasing the firmness
in those muscles, as so much happens in so small a space. This awareness of the separate use of muscles is something to bear very much
in mind.

EXERCISES

1 Lie on the floor on your back with your buttocks flat. Feel the back
as spread as possible.

Crook your knees up a little apart, aware of them pointing to the
ceiling. This should help to get your back flat. Do not push it down
by tensing, however, just get it as flat as you can.

Try to be aware of your back spreading over the floor, and not
sinking down into it. Let it spread.

Let the shoulders spread, try to feel the shoulder joints easing out,
and not cramped in. It helps if you allow the elbows to fall away from
the body, with the wrists inwards as in the diagram below.

Now think of your back lengthening along the floor — become aware
of your spine and try to feel each vertebra slightly easing away from
the other.

Feel this right to the base of the spine — to the tail in fact.

Allow the head to lengthen out of the back.

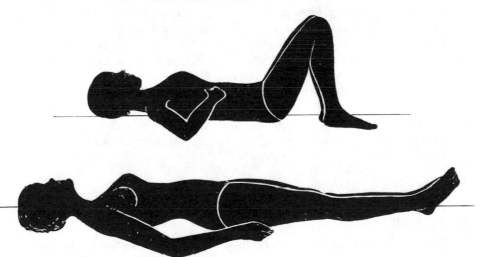

Shake your wrists, very gently, and let them drop.

Move your elbows, feel them free, and let them drop.

Turn the head easily from side to side, feeling the muscles free, then back to a central position.

Press the head back slightly into the floor, then free it, and feel the difference between the tension and relaxation in the neck muscles.

Tense the chin slightly down and then free it, again being aware of the difference.

The head should be neither pressed back nor forward — but free.

Take time to feel these sensations of lengthening and widening and freedom in the different sets of muscles. Actually say to yourself:

Back spread
Shoulders spread and free
Lengthen down to the bottom of the spine, and feel the wholeness
    of the back
Wrists free
Elbows free
Neck free, and lengthening out of the back

It is surprising how the muscles will react to these orders, and I shall give you an example to make this clear. Suppose that I asked you to span an octave on the piano with your fingers. If you prepared to do it but stopped before you actually did it you would feel the muscles in your fingers react; they would be tingling in the act of preparation and their position would be slightly different as a result. You would feel the sensation of the fingers widening without it actually happening. Obviously the fingers are much more aware than the back, and more sensitive, but the same thing happens with the back.

The important thing is not to do anything, because that will make tension. Just allow the muscles to react to the orders.

In this position, without the responsibility of keeping upright, you can be acutely aware of muscular tension and of muscular freedom.

Maintain this awareness of freedom through the following breathing exercises. Never mind stopping the breathing exercises to reaffirm this freedom.

2 Put the backs of your hands on the bottom of the rib cage, where the ribs bulge most, in fact, because that is where you will find most movement.

a Breathe in through the nose, feeling the ribs opening out along the floor at the back. Sigh out through an open mouth and throat, pushing *all* the air out of the lungs, down to the last bit. Wait until you feel the muscles between the ribs having to move, then fill slowly in again, aware of the ribs widening round the back and sides and feeling the air filling the lungs deep down. Use the floor to help the feeling of widening. Sigh out.

Do this only two or three times, but breathing in through the nose and out through an open mouth and throat. Concentrate on the capacity of breath; to this end breathing in through the nose helps to stimulate the intake.

Try not to let the upper part of the chest move, but do not worry unduly if it does, as the movement will gradually cut out the more you concentrate on the lower part of the ribs, and the freer they get. On the other hand, do not fill to such an extent that you get a feeling of tightness in the upper chest.

b   Breathe in slowly and easily, hold a moment, make sure the shoulders and neck are free, and then breathe out slowly to ten counts (by that I mean counting in your head, not aloud). It is vital to feel the muscles between the ribs controlling the outgoing air — this is the main point of the exercise. Breathing out should be quite noiseless as the throat should be open. If there is noise in the throat, however, it means that you are controlling the breath there by a certain constriction, which means there is a concentration of energy there, and when you come to vocalize there will be tension. Always wait before you breathe in again so that you feel the muscles between the ribs needing to move.

To begin with, this exercise should be done for five minutes at the least, increasing the outgoing count to fifteen. It is a lengthy exercise, but almost the most important, because, by breathing out slowly and waiting before you breathe in, the muscles spring out of their own accord. They feel the need to move, so you do not have to push them — the energy is in them.

So far you have opened up the ribs. Now you want to extend the area into the deepest part of the lungs, into the stomach. This you can do by exercising the diaphragm, which is the sheet of muscle separating the chest from the abdomen.

When the diaphragm contracts and descends breath is drawn into the lowest part of the lungs. As it relaxes and comes up so the air is expelled. You cannot feel the diaphragm directly, but you can feel the muscles at the top of the stomach which it displaces when it moves down.

25

c Breathe in all the way round so you feel the ribs open — check that the neck and shoulders are free. Put one hand on the abdominal muscles just above the waist and give a very small sigh from there (like a pant, but not sudden or jerky), and then fill in again. Do this several times so you feel the breath going in and out quite specifically to the base of the lungs.

d As with the last exercise, breathe in all the way round, put your hand on the front, and give a small sigh. Breathe in again and sigh out on 'ER' with a slight 'H' in front of the vowel, vocalizing it. Touch the sound off with the breath like a drum. Repeat several times to make quite sure where the sound is starting. Then progress on to a more sustained vowel, 'AH', holding on to it a little longer. Then even more sustained on 'AY' and 'I', first with a talking inflection and then singing them on a comfortable note. Then go back to touching them off quite shortly again — 'AH', 'AY' and 'I' — joining the breath to the sound. They should be one.

e Now put this into practice on words. A few lines of poetry are best, something that you know, but use the same principle on a piece of text. The following verse of Shakespeare is a good example of what I mean:

> Fear no more the heat o' the sun,
>   Nor the furious winter's rages;
> Thou thy worldly task hast done,
>   Home art gone, and ta'en thy wages;
> Golden lads and girls all must,
> As chimney-sweepers, come to dust.

Breathe after every second line, taking time to feel the breath go right down and the sound come out. You reach down for the sound, the chest contributes to its vibrations, and physically it is a whole sound. To begin with the sound may not root down completely — there is often a time-lag between getting the breathing working and the sound actually springing from there. You can help this by alternating a short sigh out, then breathe in, then speak two lines of the text. The important thing is to become familiar with the feeling of the sound springing from the diaphragm.

Here you have separated the diaphragm breath from the rib breath, but only for the purpose of being aware of each set of muscles. In fact they both work together, and freedom of the lower ribs helps the movement of the diaphragm. I should like to make it quite clear that I do not believe that you should work keeping the two movements separate — that is, holding the ribs out firmly and only using the breath from the diaphragm, what has been known as rib-reserve

26

breathing. To me this is unreal and makes for a great deal of tension. To make good sound it is essential that both sets of muscles are working at their best, but interrelated and free. The ribs give the solidity, the feeling that you can sit back on your voice, and the diaphragm breath makes you aware of its particular rooting.

f   Lie still for a moment, affirming the sense of length and width in the back. When you feel ready roll over on to your side and stand up, but do it quite slowly and keeping the sense of openness in the back. Stand still a moment, to notice the feeling of your back.

3   Get a stool or chair without arms on which you can sit straight but comfortably. Sit with your buttocks well down to cut out any hollowing in the back. Try to recall the sensation you had on the floor of the back long and wide. Give yourself the same orders:

>Back wide
>Back lengthen right through from the bottom of the spine
>Head lengthening out of the back — feel it as all one unit.

Head
Drop your head forward, without letting your shoulders go, and pull up slowly, feeling the muscles in the back of the neck pulling it up.

Drop back and then lift, feeling your head lifting as you do so.

Drop to one side, stretch gently, and lift.

Drop to the other side, stretch, and lift.

Drop your head forward, roll round to the side, right back, to the other side, and then drop forward.

Repeat this movement, but rolling round the other way. Be careful not to turn the head as you roll — this is cheating.

Hold the head in a normal position again. Tense it very slightly back, feeling the tension in the muscles at the back of the neck, then free it and feel the difference.

Tense your chin slightly down, again feeling where the tension comes, release it and notice the difference.

From this upright position nod very gently, noticing the freedom in the muscles of the neck and feeling the head poised but not tense. Free in fact. This exercise really is the most useful thing you can do to get the sense of freedom.

Give a very small head roll, hardly moving, but as if the head were on ball-bearings on top of the spine. Then hold it still and notice how it feels, but do not fix it. Still but not fixed.

27

Shoulders

Lift your shoulders gently, about half an inch, then drop them. When you have dropped them let them go even more — they usually can. Repeat this two or three times. Then just let them sit there — and remember that feeling of ease.

The above exercises should be done quietly, so that you can take time to notice the feeling of freedom, so that you can remember it easily and thus recapture it. I think violent muscular exercises are not particularly useful, in that they only make you conscious of the extreme conditions of tension and passive relaxation, which is a negative condition. What you want to become familiar with is the feeling of freedom which is always alert, familiar enough to be able to recall it when you want it, without the anxiety and desperation of thinking 'I must relax'. For instance, if I told you to clench your fist you would not have to think how to do it, you would be able to do it automatically, and it is this same kind of familiarity we need in relation to relaxation. There is no spectacular difference in the feelings; it should just be that the shoulders and neck feel comfortable and easy. It should feel easier and more pleasant, and therefore normal, and this should be the feeling you refer to while doing all the voice exercises.

I think it is as well to do these relaxation exercises sitting down, but the following breathing exercises can be done either sitting or standing, whichever you feel inclined to do. However, when you stand, take time to recall the feeling of your back long and wide.

4 a Put your hands up behind your head, and let your elbows be wide; to prevent tension as much as possible put the tips of your fingers on your ears to avoid pushing your head forward. This is a slightly tense position, so you have to keep as relaxed as possible — its advantage is that it opens out the rib cage. Breathe in fairly slowly through your nose, trying not to lift your shoulders. Open your mouth and sigh out — right out — and wait. Feel the need to breathe in, and in again slowly and out in the same way. Do this two or three times only, because it is tiring and tension comes quickly, but you will find it helps enormously to get the ribs moving.

b Put the backs of your hands on your ribs, with elbows and ribs as loose as possible; you should be able to feel the ribs quite firmly, and it is useful to put one hand round the back sometimes so you can feel the back ribs opening. This is the same as the breathing exercise on the floor, though of course it is more difficult to keep relaxed, and also more difficult to feel the back widening, which is so vital.

Breathe in for three counts, hold a moment and check shoulders and

28

neck. Open your mouth and breathe out for ten counts. Wait until you feel the ribs needing to move and breathe in again, and so on. Remain conscious of the muscles between the ribs controlling the outgoing air, because it is those muscles you want to stimulate, and always wait for the feeling of those muscles wanting to spring out before you take in air again. When you are ready increase the count to fifteen. In the change-over between breathing in and breathing out there should be no holding in the throat, as this means you are controlling the breath there instead of by the rib muscles — it should be those which are holding the breath. Similarly, there should be no noise in the throat when you are breathing out for the same reason. Be conscious of the air being drawn deep into the lungs.

This is the basic exercise for strengthening and freeing the ribs, so that we may eventually use all that space to contribute to the sound and give it solidity. As I have said, you can do it sitting or standing; it is also good to do it walking about, as this helps to break the tension.

c Again, this is the same as the exercise on the floor. Put one hand on your abdominal muscles above the waist, so that you feel the result of the movement of the diaphragm. Breathe in all the way round, trying particularly to get it open at the back. Give a little sigh out from the diaphragm — like a pant but not violent or sudden — repeat several times until you are sure of that feeling. It does not matter if the ribs move, so long as you get a general feeling of them being open. Then vocalize on that diaphragm breath with a little 'ER', just touching the sound off like a drum. This should be unforced yet firm, and quite specific as to the place where the sound is being made. The throat should be quite open, as that is the one place you should never feel effort. Now sustain the sound a little more by vocalizing on 'AH', and then hold it a little longer on 'AY' and 'I', getting the vowels open.

Now sing out on those two vowels, sustaining them for three counts on a comfortable note. Then go back to saying them quite shortly.

Keep that feeling of joining breath to sound.

Now put it into practice on a piece of text that you know, or the following Shakespeare song. At this point do not take too long a phrase on one breath. The aims now are to become familiar with the feeling of air going into the deepest part of the lungs and to get a very specific sound coming out, to root the sound with a clear, economical breath. Take time to let the whole cycle work.

Fear no more the heat o' the sun,
   Nor the furious winter's rages;
Thou thy worldly task hast done,
   Home art gone, and ta'en thy wages;
Golden lads and girls all must,
As chimney-sweepers, come to dust.

Fear no more the frown o' the great,
   Thou art past the tyrant's stroke;
Care no more to clothe and eat;
   To thee the reed is as the oak:
The sceptre, learning, physic, must
All follow this, and come to dust.

Fear no more the lightning-flash,
   Nor the all-dreaded thunder-stone;
Fear not slander, censure rash;
   Thou hast finish'd joy and moan:
All lovers young, all lovers must
Consign to thee, and come to dust.

No exorciser harm thee!
Nor no witchcraft charm thee!
Ghost unlaid forbear thee!
Nothing ill come near thee!
Quiet consummation have;
And renowned be thy grave!

To begin with breathe after every second line, and when that is easy breathe at every fourth line.

d   This exercise needs space because you are going to swing your arms from one side to the other. Standing up, put your arms as high as you can to one side and swing right down, letting your head and neck go completely, and swing up to the other side. The important thing is to feel as much weight as possible when you swing down, which impels the movement up to the other side, and to let your head and neck go completely – do not try to hold on to them at all. Do this once to get the idea of the movement. Next time, breathe in as you take your hands up, and as you swing down let the breath out and vocalize the vowel 'AY' quite loudly. Then up to the other side, breathing in, and swing down vocalizing the vowel 'I', so that the energy as you swing down impels the sound out. Do this at an easy pace about six times, the important thing being to feel the weight. Then do it several times singing out on those vowels on a comfortable note.

Rest a moment and then repeat the exercise, speaking the first stanza of the Shakespeare song and taking a line a swing and breathing when you get up to one side. Then immediately, without taking time to collect yourself, speak it in a normal standing position. You will find that the resulting sound is enormously free. You can increase the length of phrase as you become more familiar with the exercise.

This is a marvellous exercise for freeing sound very quickly, and you can use it on any piece of text that is useful to you. What it does is this: because you are moving quite forcefully you are actually having to take in more breath, because you are moving from the waist the breath is going down there, and because you are dropping over so completely that there can be no strain in the neck or shoulders the sound is quite free of tension.

With this exercise you experience freedom and resonance, and a feeling of the whole mechanism coming together. The more familiar you become with that experience, the more readily you will be able to call on it.

You will find that is is always valuable to speak text while doing quite strenuous, yet disciplined, movement. Any movement exercise you know will do, as well as skipping, star jumps, swinging something heavy round above your head (providing you have room), bouncing a ball, and so on — in fact, whatever you can think of in the space you have available. The movement itself makes you breathe more freely and releases you physically; it also has the advantage of taking the concentration away from the voice — the over-concentration — and so allows the voice to take on textures that are not consciously produced, very often releasing quite rich sound and different rhythms in the process. It is rather like learning to ride a bicycle: to begin with you hold on too tight and you are unable to balance properly, and it is only when you relax that balance becomes natural. However, this releasing must not be done without good, solid exercises first.

It is always a good thing to do the exercises and speak any text you are using while you are walking about, sitting down, bending over, stretching, and so on, so that the exercises do not become synonymous with standing still. Sometimes beat your chest while speaking to feel the vibrations there.

As this is a breathing exercise for which you happen to be using words it does not matter whether the phrasing is quite right or the meaning complete. You are using it as a bridge between just doing exercises and applying the breathing to words. What does matter is that you take time to experience the whole breathing process so that it becomes familiar and easy, and so will become the norm and therefore feel right when you are actually doing something in which you are totally involved. To begin with you will be over-conscious of the muscular action and may force too much breath out, but this

31

will ease off as you become sure of what you are doing, and eventually your breathing will become quite normal.

To recap, then. You have opened the rib cage by stimulating particularly the muscles between the ribs, by waiting for them to need to move, so that they spring out of their own volition and not by you pushing them out. You have also felt the back widening as you do so. You have drawn the air into the deepest part of the lungs, conscious of the spine lengthening down to its root as you do so. You have also been conscious of air being drawn in through the nose, down through the bronchial tubes and the bronchioles to fill the space in the lungs. You have felt the air going deep into the stomach as the diaphragm goes down, and felt some movement of the stomach muscles to allow for this. And you have used all this resource to make sound, using the Shakespeare song or something that you like particularly which can serve the same purpose and sounds good. You have done it standing still and moving about.

The firmness produced by these exercises does not make the tone heavy, as some people think; on the contrary, it makes it more buoyant and opens up the range. It should make the upper notes just as free as the lower notes, and just as accessible. When you first start doing the exercises you will probably unconsciously keep the voice to the lower part of your range, because one tends to associate a lower pitch with a richer tone, but you will soon progress beyond this and find that the notes over the whole range become equally rich and free.

It can be extremely useful to work on these exercises with other people, particularly for breathing. If you can get someone to put their hands on your ribs at the back — the two thumbs on the spine and the whole hand spreading out to press firmly on the muscles at the back and sides of the ribs — you can then feel the movement of the ribs much more specifically, and without the confusing tensions of having to keep your own hands on your ribs, which does have a tendency to make the shoulders lift a bit. Another person can also check the tensions you may get in the shoulders and neck while breathing. The reciprocal action is very valuable indeed, as an awareness of another person's breathing mechanism and muscular tensions helps you to pinpoint your own movements.

The next step is to apply this breathing to quite demanding pieces of text, something in which you are not particularly emotionally involved but which goes further to bridge the gap between exercise and interpretation. Narrative and descriptive material is best, as this demands plenty of range but keeps a conversational use of the range, thus stopping you becoming at all rhetorical. As you progress so you can use more complicated and more emotionally loaded material. The following two passages make very good starting-points. The Shakespeare is liquid and is not difficult to speak. It is very relaxed, your voice doing the work of a film camera setting the scene. The description is very particular, and so asks for a lot of different vocal texture. It sounds good, and so it helps you to make good sound. If you do something very ordinary it would be false to make it sound good, and at this point you are after the experience of good sound. The phrasing of the Milton is not easy, the sentences are inverted and long, it has a big sound, and it requires good, sustained breathing. I have marked where to breathe, as it is helpful to do so at this initial stage so that you can concentrate on the mechanics of the breathing, but as it gets easier you make your own choice of phrase.

Take them both purely at a story level. I do not think it matters taking good material for exercises, provided that you are aware of the level at which you are using them. It is always so much more interesting to use good material, and you are likely to learn so much more from it. Keep them narrative and the range flexible and colloquial. You are using them as an extension of the breathing exercises, so:

i.   Check that your position is good.
ii. Check the freedom in your neck and shoulders.
iii. Take plenty of time to breathe. Let the ribs be open and flexible to start with, get the diaphragm working, and test the sound springing off it by sighing out and vocalizing on a vowel.
iv. Feel the throat quite open — this is the one place where you should feel no effort.
v.   Root the sound.

Chorus:

Now entertain conjecture of a time/
When creeping murmur and the poring dark
Fills the wide vessel of the universe./
From camp to camp, through the foul womb of night,
The hum of either army stilly sounds,/
That the fixed sentinels almost receive
The secret whispers of each other's watch./
Fire answers fire, and through their paly flames
Each battle sees the other's umber'd face./
Steed threatens steed, in high and boastful neighs,

Piercing the night's dull ear;/ and from the tents
The armourers, accomplishing the knights,
With busy hammers closing rivets up,
Give dreadful note of preparation./
The country cocks do crow, the clocks do toll,
And the third hour of drowsy morning name./
Proud of their numbers, and secure in soul,
The confident and over-lusty French
Do the low-rated English play at dice,/
And chide the cripple tardy-gaited night
Who, like a foul and ugly witch doth limp
So tediously away./ The poor condemned English,
Like sacrifices, by their watchful fires
Sit patiently, and inly ruminate
The morning's danger;/ and their gesture sad,
Investing lank-lean cheeks and war-worn coats.
Presenteth them unto the gazing moon
So many horrid ghosts./ O now, who will behold
The royal Captain of this ruined band
Walking from watch to watch, from tent to tent,/
Let him cry, 'Praise and glory on his head!'/
For forth he goes and visits all his host,/
Bids them good morrow with a modest smile,
And calls them brothers, friends, and countrymen./
Upon his royal face there is no note
How dread an army hath enrounded him,/
Nor doth he dedicate one jot of colour
Unto the weary and all-watchèd night,/
But freshly looks, and overbears attaint
With cheerful semblance and sweet majesty;/
That every wretch, pining and pale before,
Beholding him, plucks comfort from his looks:/
A largess universal like the sun,
His liberal eye doth give to every one,
Thawing cold fear, that mean and gentle all
Behold,/ as may unworthiness define,
A little touch of Harry in the night./
And so our scene must to the battle fly;/
Where — O for pity! — we shall much disgrace,
With four or five most vile and ragged foils,
Right ill-disposed in brawl ridiculous,
The name of Agincourt./ Yet sit and see,
Minding true things by what their mockeries be.

Henry V, Act iv, Prologue

From *SAMSON AGONISTES*

Messenger: Occasions drew me early to this City,/
And as the gates I entered with Sun-rise,
The Morning Trumpets Festival proclaimed
Through each high street:/ little I had dispatch't
When all abroad was rumour'd that this day
Samson should be brought forth to show the people
Proof of his mighty strength in feats and games;/
I sorrow'd at his captive state, but minded
Not to be absent at that spectacle./
The building was a spacious Theatre
Half round on two main Pillars vaulted high,/
With seats where all the Lords and each degree
Of sort, might sit in order to behold,/
The other side was op'n, where the throng
On banks and scaffolds under Skie might stand;/
I among these aloof obscurely stood./
The Feast and noon grew high, and Sacrifice
Had fill'd their hearts with mirth, high cheer, and wine,
When to their sports they turn'd./ Immediately
Was Samson as a public servant brought,
In their state Livery clad;/ before him Pipes
And Timbrels, on each side went armed guards,
Both horse and foot before him and behind,
Archers, and Slingers, Cataphracts and Spears./
At sight of him the people with a shout
Rifted the Air clamouring their god with praise,
Who had made their dreadful enemy their thrall./
He patient but undaunted where they led him,
Came to the place,/and what was set before him
Which without help of eye might be assay'd,
To heave, pull, draw, or break,/he still perform'd
All with incredible, stupendious force,
None daring to appear Antagonist./
At length for intermission sake they led him
Between the pillars;/ he his guide requested
(For so from such as nearer stood we heard)/
As over-tir'd to let him lean a while
With both his arms on those two massie Pillars
That to the arched roof gave main support./
He unsuspicious led him; which when Samson
Felt in his arms, with head awhile inclin'd,
And eyes fast fix'd he stood,/as one who pray'd,
Or some great matter in his mind revolv'd./

35

At last with head erect thus cried aloud, /
'Hitherto, Lords, what your commands impos'd
I have perform'd, as reason was, obeying,
Not without wonder or delight beheld. /
Now of my own accord such other trial
I mean to show you of my strength, yet greater; /
As with amaze shall strike all who behold.' /
This utter'd, straining all his nerves, he bow'd; /
As with the force of winds and waters pent,
When Mountains tremble, those two massie Pillars,
With horrible convulsion to and fro,
He tugg'd, he shook, till down they came/and drew
The whole roof after them, with burst of thunder
Upon the heads of all who sat beneath/
Lords, Ladies, Captains, Councillors, or Priests, /
Their choice nobility and flower, not only
Of this but each Philistian City round
Met from all parts to solemnize this Feast. /
Samson with these immixt, inevitably
Pull'd down the same destruction on himself. /
The vulgar only scaped who stood without.

John Milton

Start by being very particular about your state of freedom and the
application of the breath. As you begin to feel at ease with the
breathing and relaxation stop for a little while. Talk part of the text
very quietly, not being conscious of the breath, but now beginning to
explore the progression of the narrative through the particular words
and images that are used. Take a phrase at a time, but not speaking
any word until you are sure of its meaning and image to you. Just
tell it. When you have talked a part of it through very quietly,
receiving the images, go back to thinking about the breathing and try
to find the thought and the breath together, so that the thought is
also coming from your centre and you are rooting your thought as
well as your breath.

Each person's needs will be different, of course, and you have to
rely on your own judgment, but in fact you have to work from both
ends, as it were. The voice cannot open out and be responsive unless
the muscles are ready. At the same time it is no good the muscles
being ready unless your thought and sensibility are alive. You are
therefore working for the two to be together, and so you use all the
means you can to get them rooted together.

To open the sound, use the same means as I gave for the
Shakespeare song, particularly the exercise of swinging down and

letting the head and neck go. This exercise is the most valuable, but all the suggestions I made should be used to obtain the freedom you are after.

If you get a lot of tension, and if you are particularly inclined to push with the head or make small physical movements in the effort of getting the sound out (physically beating it out, as it were), practise a good deal lying on the floor. In that position you can isolate much more easily the right kind of tension from the wrong kind, and you are freer to concentrate on using the breath. Try quite long pieces of text in that position, and notice when you want to move and where, and consciously relax. These involuntary tense movements are difficult to overcome, and the process requires patience. Take plenty of time, and do not become cross with yourself. It helps to think in terms of making all that energy into sound.

All tension comes from anxiety to please, and eventually you have to come round to the view quite simply that what you have to offer is good enough.

I have purposely varied the length of phrase in these two pieces of text, firstly because you want to be able to take in small breaths easily and quickly, and secondly because you also want to be able to sustain solid sound over a fair length of phrase without any feeling that you are going to run out. This, of course, has to do with your thought; if you are aware of the weight of your thought you will find you have enough breath to reach, at least it's fifty-fifty each way!

You now have a general basis for work which gives a good progression, the benefit of which is cumulative. Once you begin to get a sense of vocal freedom and you begin to hear new notes in your voice, then the work becomes more interesting and you want to go on. Once you begin to trust the voice and have confidence in it, so the possibilities open up and a lot of the faults disappear because they are no longer necessary. You can now adapt and extend the exercises as given to meet bigger demands, or to cope with specific limitations. In particular, you want to be able to increase the volume without losing timbre, to make a low volume carry, and to increase the textual richness and range.

Let us see how you can use the basic exercises to do these things.

1 First of all you must find out how to increase the musical texture of the sound, and perhaps find more weight. When people complain that a voice is too high it seldom has much to do with pitch — it is nearly always that the resonators in the chest are not reinforcing the sound, with the result that it sounds like playing the melody on a piano without any bass notes. This sounds high, but as soon as you put the bass chords in the whole thing sounds an octave lower. It is

the same with the voice: you have the note, but the more completely the resonators back it the richer and more surprising it will be.

The solidity, the undertones and the richness will come with the opening up of the ribs together with the relaxation of the neck, for if the neck is tense to any degree it will cut out the chest notes. The greatest source of confidence you have is the strength of the lower ribs at the back. The strength and openness there gives you a sense of being able to 'sit' on the tone, and gives you a feeling that the sound belongs to your weight – and the more whole the sound the more complete will be the belief in it. It has nothing to do with what might be called 'actorish' tone because it is unforced and uncontrived.

a Do plenty of work in the floor position, speaking text, using the floor to feel the ribs open and to feel the voice vibrating on the floor.

b Lie on the floor on your front, feeling very spread over the floor, with your head turned to one side. Speak some text in that position, again being conscious of the vibration through the chest on to the floor. Hum in that position.

c Speak a part of your text while standing with your hands behind your head, so that the ribs are open.

d Sing out on 'AY' and 'I' on a comfortable note, with your hands gently beating your chest to feel the vibrations.

e Sing part of your text on one note (that is, intone it), such as the first fifteen lines of the Milton, slowly and firmly. Then speak it. The sustained breathing you need when singing helps to open out the sound. However, always end up by speaking it with quite ordinary talking inflections. Do this on different pitches, always keeping the throat open.

f Do the same as in the last exercise, only sing it as a piece of recitative, so that it is very large and rhythmically well marked. This is very helpful if you have a long speech, because singing it in this way makes the rhythms more marked so that when you come to talk it, you will find the rhythm more interesting even though it is a lot more subtle.

g Jog very heavily, either round the room or in one spot, feeling a great weight as you jog, and speak while you are doing this. Do it for several minutes, then stop and speak it ordinarily; the weight and relaxation will hold into the speaking.

2 Secondly, you must discover how to increase volume without tension. One of the most common traps for the actor is that he confuses volume with size. Size of feeling and size of character has more to do

with time and weight than volume. The exercises which you have already done will have made you find tone which, of itself, has weight and size. Nor is volume itself a way of being heard. A quiet voice can carry well, and I have sat through loud performances without actually hearing anything. Volume itself is not important for anyone can shout. Nevertheless, there are times when you need to call on something really big and, certainly, you need to know that the volume is there if you want it. But it should always be used with discretion as if you cannot suppress it any longer — like steam being held back. When you let out that volume you must never lose the clarity of speech because then the specific reason for the size will not be present. With increased volume you always need increased pressure of consonants as there is much more sound to cut up into words. This process is quite logical.

Basically what is required is a voice which is big enough to share in whatever area you have to share it. This has to do with your own reaching out as a person, in particular with allowing time, for the sound has to travel further. You need to know that you can call on great volume when there is a real reason for it. Volume for its own sake is tiring for the listener. There is always that hang-over from being told to 'speak up' which is somehow inseparable from the idea of speaking higher and the misconception that a higher pitch carries further. If you use more volume there is a great danger that you send the pitch up; the neck then becomes tight, the normal talking inflection disappears and the result is a pressure of sound which does not convey meaning and which has all the undertones ironed out. Never forget that the text itself contains the size, the breadth of what you are saying coming largely from the energy contained in your text.

In practice you can work on increasing volume by starting comfortably and gradually getting louder, very consciously keeping relaxed and retaining normal talking pitch.

a   Lie on the floor and loosen up, with the ribs and diaphragm working freely. In particular, concentrate on keeping the neck and shoulders free. Speak lines of text quietly to begin with, gradually increasing the volume but making sure you keep the key of the pitch the same. Stay quite conversational but resolve the inflections down to the same bass note — that is, use plenty of inflection but do not pitch the text up as a whole.

b   Repeat this standing up and moving. Speak text conversationally, steadily increasing the volume and keeping the range free with plenty of upper notes, and the words sharp and specific. Keep the neck absolutely free and open and find the energy from your centre. You have, therefore, to centre the thought and find its weight. When you start to get tense, stop, get free and then continue.

c   Try the same exercise, singing and stretching your arms while you do so.

3   The next problem to deal with is breathiness, both general breathy tone and breathy attack where you use all the breath at the beginning of a phrase and cannot sustain the tone to the end of the phrase. In these cases you are not making all your breath into sound. This comes from basic anxiety to give to an audience; but you are not being specific in the sound you are giving and are, therefore, wasting a good deal of energy. Physically it is caused by a lack of muscular firmness in the ribs and diaphragm – the ribs usually collapse very quickly. All the singing exercises are useful and the following exercises also help.

a   Exercise quite a lot with your hands behind your head. Be as relaxed as possible and take care not to push the head forward. Start speaking text with your hands in that position, gradually bringing them down as you speak.

b   It is valuable sometimes to reverse the timing of the rib exercises so that you breathe in over a long count of 10 or 15, and out for a short count of 3 or 6.

c   Keeping the ribs as open as possible, though not at all rigid, reach for your deep diaphragm breath and sing out smoothly on 'M' for 6, 8 and 10 counts, increasing the count out as it becomes easy and smooth. Focus the 'M' on an object quite a distance away and imagine your note to be a thread going out of your mouth and attaching itself to that object. This helps to keep the sound very smooth. Do this exercise with the vowels 'OO', 'OH', 'AH', 'AY' and 'I' as well as with 'M'.

d   With the ribs open and reaching down for the breath sing out on 'M' and on the vowels, focusing the sound at different distances; start on something very close to you and gradually increase the distance. As the sound goes further do not let it get louder; let it travel further by the increase in its density and firmness not by volume. Be careful that the pitch does not get higher. Be quite precise about the object on which you are focusing and make the sound fill the distance. You should notice a difference in the quality of the sound.

When the attack is breathy so that you burst out at the beginning of phrases and run out of breath before the end the same exercises apply. This is a limiting fault because it dictates a rhythm. It means that you can choose how to inflect and time words at the beginning

40

of a phrase but you do not have the same freedom for the end.
The possibilities of meaning cannot, therefore, be truly investigated.
The result is also rhythmically repetitive. You can add to these
exercises:

e Go through a text making the phrases you tackle on one breath
unnaturally long, afterwards cutting the length down to normal
speech phrasing.

f Experiment by intentionally stressing and elongating the last word
in a phrase: you can even sing it. Though this stress will not
necessarily be right, it opens up possible ways of stressing and
inflecting that you cannot be aware of when you are breath-bound.
It is very interesting to do this and it breaks your rhythm pattern.
As soon as the exercises become interesting you will find that you
automatically have enough breath.

g Another valuable exercise for finding firm, unforced tone is to
literally throw vowels. Imagine you have a ball in your hand which
you are going to throw at a particular place — be quite clear about
the aim. As you release the ball you will release sound by singing a
vowel. 'AY' and 'I' are good vowels to take as they are so open.
Imagine a ball in your hand, lift your arm and as you do so breathe
in. Throw the ball to the place chosen; as you throw release the
sound and throw the vowel, letting it follow the imaginary ball so
sustaining the sound until you have reached your object. You will
hear that the resultant sound is firm and clear. This helps both
breathy and glottal attack for it assists co-ordination of breath and
sound.

4 Overbalance of head resonance is a complicated problem because,
as I said earlier, it often conflicts with your own judgment and ear
and you sometimes have to rely on someone else's opinion. It
happens when there is strong head resonance (that is, sinus tone
and resonance in the bones of the head and face) which is not
balanced sufficiently by the lower resonances from the chest and
neck. Head resonance has its own edge, brilliance and carrying power,
and makes the voice seem easy to manoeuvre. However, it will
always sound curiously disembodied and a little contrived unless it is
balanced by true and warm chest notes. In fact, it means that the
voice will not have the reality because you are not really reaching
down for it, rooting it or centring it. If it is not based it has a
metallic quality and lacks dimension. It is therefore a limited voice.
The difficulty here is that the voice feels so sure that when you
release it and get the lower chest notes it does not sound so firm to
yourself. As I have said, this can be the result of training the voice for
singing where the emphasis is put on all the possible resonating spaces

without relating the sound specifically to the actor's need to express himself. To get the balance right is a matter of adjusting where the sound should spring from and also of releasing the soft palate so that the undertones are allowed to play their part.

To release the soft palate, exercise the back of the tongue and back of the palate by saying 'ge, ge, ge' so that you become aware of the muscles involved. Then press the tongue up to the palate quite hard and say 'ge', lingering on the consonant. Then consciously drop the back of the tongue and palate, with the jaw open, noticing how they are very relaxed and heavy. Do this again, consciously tensing the tongue so that the sound is hard and tight; then drop the palate and tongue and say 'ge' with them both quite relaxed; then open and say 'AH' keeping the tongue and palate absolutely free. Feel this freedom in the back of the throat for a moment. Then breathe in and gently vocalize 'AH', 'AY' and 'I' on a deep diaphragm breath. Now breathe in and speak a few lines of text, keeping the feeling of openness in the throat and making sure the breath starts the sound. You will then feel all the area in the back of the throat open and contributing to the sound. Take time over this exercise for it makes a great deal of difference to your sound.

5 Inflection and use of range must always come from the specific attitude to your text. However, you can increase the flexibility of range by experimenting with pieces of text that require different pitches, and by consciously making yourself key them at different places in your range. Always keep the throat free and the breath well rooted, reinforcing the sound at all levels. You will find that when you use the lower notes you will need to be more conscious of the diction and that when you use the higher notes you have to consciously sustain the chest resonance.

6 Glottal attack is usually ironed out by the exercises already given. However, if it is very persistent take different vowels, singing and then speaking them. First precede them with 'H', then just think the 'H' but do not actually say it. Try to find a firm, open attack.

Thus, you reach down for the sound; it is touched off like a drum; it releases itself without conscious mental effort and reaches as far as you wish. It is given resonance by the whole body. The sound is there to back the word. If you practise the breathing exercises sufficiently you will find the effortlessness you require. The audience should never feel you are using all your strength because this puts you in a position of weakness.

3 Muscularity and Word

The breath starts the sound by hitting the vocal cords when they are approximated — that is when they are drawn together — causing them to vibrate and so set up sound waves. The initial sound is then amplified and resonated through the body, and can be formed into words by the movement or articulation of the various organs of speech.

You have discovered your own vocal energy through the breathing exercises and by finding the resonating possibilities in the body. You must now transform that energy and send it out via the word, for it is this that must impinge on the listener. It is necessary to find how to link the vocal energy with the energy of the word. The next step, therefore, is to become familiar with the movement of the jaw, the lips and tongue, and the soft palate, which are the muscles we use to make vowels and consonants.

Whatever the text, the actor has to find the specific measure of the words he is using and relay them with clarity and accuracy in whatever space he is in, so that they can be heard without strain. So you have four things to deal with:

1 The basic clarity of the individual speech.
2 Adapting that clarity to the space you are using.
3 The satisfactory placing and balance of vowels and consonants, which will then add another dimension of resonance to the voice.
4 Fulfilling the intention of the word.

In one way the exercises for muscularity are easier than the breathing exercises in that you feel their benefit more immediately, and so you are quicker to feel the possibilities of the voice. Certainly, five minutes' exercise can make a tremendous difference to the awareness of what you can do. But, in another way, they are more complex because of the infinite variations of individual speech depending on environment and personality, the factors which I mentioned in the introductory chapter, and because of the fact that it is often such small adjustments that are needed. For instance, slightly too much or too little pressure on the consonants, clipping vowels, devoicing final voiced consonants, too much nasal resonance, or lack of awareness of the different length of vowels can take away from the right energy in the word. Although these are minor in themselves, they can take away from the total effect of the speech. It is so often the small things that make the difference. These small points are very often in evidence in experienced actors.

For the person with particularly unclear speech or a specific accent problem, the thing that matters is still the concentration on the right energy in the word and not on making totally standard vowels and consonants. The point is that there is no completely right way of speaking: it can only be right for the individual. You can only say that is not acceptable because it is just a little too Scots, or a little too cockney, or too 'Kensington', or that the consonants are slithering and not firm enough, or that you are not giving full value to the vowels, and so on, and therefore not communicating fully. If you were to make each sound absolutely standard the result would not necessarily sound right either because it would be too formal. The purpose is not to iron out individual characteristics or regional differences of speech. If we did this some of the natural vitality of the speech would also get ironed out. Yet, because the actor needs to be on terms with and familiar with speech other than his own, and because different texts require very accurate speech too defined an accent or too marked characteristics will limit the range of parts he can play and, of course, limit his subtlety — unless, of course, he chooses to trade on those limitations. It is a delicate balance. You have to find a basic acceptable norm of clarity which evolves out of your own speech and from which you can depart at will according to the demands of the character or text. Your first base must be to ensure that you have that common starting-point of 'acceptability'. With a reasonably good ear it is easy to make standard sounds on their own. It is, however, difficult to make them with complete rhythmical freedom so that they do not in any way hinder the subtlety of your communication. It can be as noticeable, and there-fore as limiting, to make too careful sounds as well as too slack ones. The more you do the exercises the more you will realise that it is the satisfactory use of the muscles that you must rely on, for when the muscles themselves are working right the sounds will be properly defined. You are only doing what an athlete does, and that is preparing the muscles you need to do a particular job.

Of course, the needs will vary, but at whatever point you are starting from — that is, whether you already have clear standard speech, or whether you have certain sounds that are too regional, or whether the speech is simply inadequate to carry, it is important to work through all the exercises thoroughly before you become selective, for what you are also doing is discovering the energy in the muscles you use to make vowels and consonants. It is by no means a matter of just being clear. It is also being aware of the energy and life that words have of themselves in their particular context. It is true that an actor can have a grating and inflexible voice, yet, if the right kind of energy is in the word, and by that I mean if the word collects the emotion and thought intentions and relays them, then he can be magnetic, and we are drawn to listen. It is again a two-way process: the actor informs the words with his own understanding and they can inform him if he listens to what they say. Of course the better the text the more the words tell you. The greater your awareness of the different muscular energy contained in the words the more possibilities of length, stress and weight there are. You need to investigate and know the movements of the muscles that form words so that they are firm enough to make clear vowels and consonants with exactly the right energy required, and flexible enough to respond to all the demands and nuances of speech. There are a million ways of inflecting, stressing and dwelling on any given word.

Also, by finding the energy in these muscles you will be able to adapt more easily to whatever space you are using. Whether in a large theatre or in a small studio the vocal projection of your thought and feeling depends on this clarity of the word, its absolute right energy and its timing. Obviously what is happening to your body is part of this. Words collect emotional and physical responses. You will find that a large space requires more weight and friction on a consonant, so you will need fractionally longer consonants the further the sound has to carry. Also, and this is very important, the more vocal power you are using the more quantity of consonant you need to break the tone up into words. The richer the tone the more bite we need on the consonant; therefore, a thin tone requires little consonant for the word to carry and be clear. This is easy to understand if you think of speaking in a stone building such as a church. If you increase the volume you confuse the speech, but if you increase the amount of consonant then the speech is clear. It is the muscular energy in words that allows you to take the volume down to a minimal level and yet still be heard. Finding this energy takes away much of the anxiety of simply being heard and so it takes the stress away from vocal power which alone is valuable. On the other hand, in a studio you need great precision and control, dwelling as little as possible on sounds. With little volume you require great elasticity of the normal speaking range which is quite difficult. The muscles, therefore, have to be extra sensitive so that sound can be specific and have bite yet display little muscular movement. The naturalism required can so often lead to dull speaking.

When you get the right energy and control in these muscles you will find that the words spring out without effort and of their own volition. You will then be free to alight on words and to extend them or sharpen them as you wish. A great deal of inaudibility of speech comes from bad timing in the making of vowels and consonants rather than from a lack of forming them.

You must now discover where to find this energy. Before looking at consonants in relation to this, I should like, briefly, to clarify what a consonant is.

45

A *consonant* is a sound in which the passage of air or sound is stopped or partially stopped by either the lips or parts of the tongue. For some consonants the soft palate is involved, and the position of the jaw is always important. When the passage of sound is completely stopped it is called a plosive, and when it is only partially stopped it is called a continuant. Take, for example, the lip consonants 'p', 'b' and 'm' — for 'p' and 'b' the lips are pressed together to stop the passage of sound for a fraction of time. They hold the sound for a moment and it is not until the lips are released that the consonant is heard with its slight explosion of breath, as for 'p', or sound as for 'b'. On the other hand, for the nasal consonant 'm', though the lips are closed to stop the sound coming out through the mouth, the soft palate is lowered to allow it to be resonated and sent out through the nose. The passage is then only partially closed and so we call it a continuant consonant because it is possible to go on making it for an indefinite length of time. The jaw for these sounds is partially open.

As you can see, consonants fall into two groups, plosive and continuant. There is also a further difference that you will have noticed and that is that they can be either voiced or breathed. If they are voiced it means that the vocal cords are approximated and vibrating. In the case of 'b' it is a voiced or vibrating sound that explodes out when the lips are released, whereas for the breathed sound 'p' the vocal cords are not drawn together and so it is purely breath that is stopped and then released. However, it must be noted that with a plosive voiced sound such as 'b' there is a fractional amount of breath that escapes on release, and this is what gives the voiced sounds a certain edge and carrying power. Of course, 'm' is a voiced sound and is particularly useful, as are all voiced continuants, in that you can feel the vibrations or the friction on the lips as you hold it, which is of particular value in placing the tone. These are, therefore, two further groups — voiced and breathed consonants.

In timing, and this is very important, consonants have three parts — the coming together of muscles, the holding and the release. Bearing these differences in mind, we will look at the muscles involved in making the other consonants.

The tip of the tongue is mainly responsible for the consonants 't', 'd', 'n' and 'l', though the whole of the tongue is involved. For the plosives 't' and 'd' the tongue-tip is pressed against the teeth ridge just behind the top teeth and the sides of the tongue are pressed up against the top gums, completely stopping the passage of sound for a fraction of time. There should be no escape of air for the time that you hold it or the consonant will be messy. As you release the tongue-tip the sound explodes out — 't' on the breath and 'd' vocalised. However, 'l' is a voiced continuant sound, for though the

46

tongue-tip is pressed against the teeth ridge stopping the sound there, the sides of the tongue are lowered to allow it to escape and continue out through the mouth; the sound is not completed until the tip is released. The quality of 'l', as you will see later, varies according to its position in a word and this difference in quality is made by the position of the back of the tongue, whether it is high or low. For 'n' the tongue is pressed up all the way round but the soft palate is lowered to allow the sound to be resonated and continue out through the nose. It is not completed until the tongue-tip is released. The jaw is partially open for these sounds.

For the consonants 'k', 'g' and 'ng' the back of the tongue is pressed against the back of the soft palate to stop the sound coming through the mouth. As we release the back of the tongue we release the consonants 'k' and 'g', but for 'ng' the soft palate is lowered to allow it its nasal resonance, and to give it its continuant value. The jaw is fairly open for these sounds. The freedom of the soft palate is particularly important for their quality; if it is tense and tight the sounds themselves will be squeezed and thin, but if the palate is free to come down to meet the back of the tongue the vibration between them is much greater and, consequently, the resonance is fuller.

'S' and 'z' are continuant consonants in which the passage of sound is channelled down the centre of the tongue. The jaw is closed and the sound escapes through the spaces in between the teeth, the placing of the tip of the tongue being variable; 's' is breathed and 'z' is voiced. It is exactly the right amount of friction between the breath or sound resulting from the pressure of the tongue and teeth that makes it precise. 'Sh' and 'ge' (the soft 'g' as in the word 'measure') are again continuant, one breathed and one voiced, formed by the sides of the tongue pressed against the gum and the blade arched high to make pressure between it and the roof of the mouth so making friction. The jaw is almost closed, and the sound is given a particular resonance by the rounding of the lips. 'Tch' and 'dg' are plosives and are, in fact, each a compression of two consonant sounds said at the same time — the breathed 't' and 'sh' said as one sound and the voiced 'd' and 'ge' the same way. Again the jaw is almost closed. 'F' (breathed) and 'v' (voiced) are made with the jaw partially open, the top teeth pressing lightly but firmly against the lower lip to make friction as the sound escapes. 'Th' is made with the jaw partially open, the tongue tip placed between the teeth which press on it just enough to make friction as the sound escapes. It can be voiced as in the word 'this' or breathed as in the word 'thin'.

All this is fairly obvious, but what matters is how much muscular activity you use: how much pressure you use to make the plosives both in their holding and their release, how much air you allow to escape on release, how much friction you allow on the continuant consonants, how much vibration you get on the voiced consonants, and how much time you take on them according to their position in the word. There is infinite variability of pressure, vibration and time.

A *vowel* is different in that it always has a free passage of sound through the mouth and it is always vocalised. It is made different by the shaping of the lips and tongue but, of course, the freedom of the jaw and the mobility of the soft palate make their own differences to the quality. Some are called pure sounds — that is, the shape through which they are made remains the same. Others are diphthongal — that is, they are two sounds glided together and spoken in the space of time it takes to speak one sound. The shape changes as you speak it. To make these standard is, of course, more complicated. Some vowels are by their nature long and some are short. In my list I will put the long ones in capital letters.

The following vowels are shaped predominantly by the lips though the position and freedom of the blade of the tongue affects their quality:

OO as in 'lose'
oo as in 'look'
OH as in 'load' (diphthongal)
AW as in 'lawn'
o as in 'lot'
OW as in 'loud' (diphthongal)
OI as in 'loin' (diphthongal)

The shape of the lips varies from being closed to being quite open and the movement on the diphthongs is quite extensive.

In the following group the tongue shapes the vowels because it goes from a flat position through different stages of arching the blade:

AH as in 'large'
u as in 'lung'
ER as in 'learn'
a as in 'lad'
e as in 'let'
AY as in 'lace' (diphthongal)
i as in 'link'
EE as in 'leaf'
I as in 'lie' (diphthongal)
EAR as in 'near' (diphthongal)
AIR as in 'hair' (diphthongal)

The important thing is the difference in length between the vowels, not merely that some are long and some are short by nature, but that within the context of different consonants and different stresses, there is infinite variability in the length. The muscular awareness in making the vowels is also important.

48

As you can see, the movements involved in making vowels and consonants are comparatively small and take place within a small area. (It is interesting to notice how little actual movement you can make while keeping the speech intelligible). Therefore, the smallest variation of placing and movement can make a relatively big difference to the speech. Because it is difficult to isolate the awareness of these muscles, you have to exercise each muscle separately in order to recognise what happens. To do this you need the jaw open to a comfortable degree and you need to keep it open. Unless you can keep it open and steady two things are likely to go wrong with the exercises: you will not be able to separate the awareness of the precise movements of the muscles of the lips and tongue from the movement of the jaw; and if the jaw is not open to a certain degree you will not be able to exercise the lips and tongue fully, so the exercises will not be properly effective. This is why it is valuable at the beginning to use a bone-prop or something similar to prop the jaw open while doing the exercises.

A bone-prop is a small prop about the thickness of a pencil, of varying lengths, which you put between the teeth to keep the jaw open and steady. It has a groove each end into which your teeth can fit to prevent it from jumping out under pressure from the jaw. They are available from John Bell and Croyden of Wigmore Street, London. However, you can find a substitute quite easily, such as a piece of cork or part of a plastic pen or toothbrush handle, cut down to the right size, but the bone-prop is more satisfactory because of the grooves.

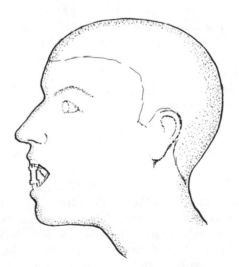

The props come in varying lengths with 1/8th of an inch in between each size. The biggest that should be used is 7/8ths of an inch and 3/4 of an inch or 5/8ths is about normal. If necessary, you can go down to a 1/2 inch one. Great care should be taken to find the right size as, obviously, too wide a one will create tension in the jaw, something which must be avoided, and too small a one will not open the jaw sufficiently to make the exercises useful. Their use varies very much with the individual, and you have to be very sensible about it.

If you can use one without setting up over-much tension in the jaw then do so, because it increases the effectiveness of the exercises enormously and the benefit is felt more quickly. It will probably feel uncomfortable but it should not make the jaw tense. If it does, do not force yourself to use it, because then tensions come in the neck and back of the tongue and that is harmful. Sometimes the set of the jaw and teeth make it difficult to use, or the teeth can be over-sensitive, or it can set up tensions in the throat which make you feel slightly sick. These are the exceptions and most people find them perfectly comfortable to use. However, if you find you cannot use a prop watch carefully in a mirror to be quite sure of what is moving and, to begin with, put a finger on each lip corner to help keep the jaw constant. It is essential to isolate the jaw movements from the movements of the other muscles.

I do stress that using a bone-prop or exaggerating the movement of the jaw has nothing to do in the end with mouthing words. It is done simply to place in your mind the exact movement of the muscles. Ultimately, when working, you should be no more aware of the mechanical process of making words than you are when talking normally in conversation with no thought of projection. There is, however, an important difference between the intention of words produced with little or no muscular movement because the muscles are not alive and words produced with little apparent muscular movement yet with the muscles alive so that the right energy is placed in them. It also makes a difference to the sound.

In these exercises it is not speed that matters. Speed will come soon enough and, in any case, you nearly always manage to find it when you want it. What matters is taking time to feel the complete action of the muscles. For instance, when exercising the tongue for the tongue-tip consonants 't', 'd', 'n' and 'l' it is the right pressure of about 1/8th of an inch of the flat of the tongue against the teeth ridge that must be found and remembered. There should not be too much pressure as the release into the vowel will be jerky which will interfere with the rhythm and also make the sound hard. Nor should there be too little pressure as then the consonant will slither and it will not have enough bite to carry. It will also not have enough vibration of its own if it is a voiced consonant and so will not contribute to the sound. The right action of the muscles not only makes the words clear but the muscles will have their own vibration, and therefore resonance, and so contribute positively to the whole sound. You can make quite clear, faultless consonants which are not breathy but which are negative in that they make no positive contribution to the resonance, and so some dimension and texture in the voice is lost. Experiment by saying the following pairs of breathed and voiced consonants, noticing the positive vibrations of the voiced ones:

p – b
t – d
k – g
s – z
f – v
th – th (voiced)
sh – ge (soft)
ch – dg

Vowels depend as much as consonants on the awareness of muscular activity for their definition, though, because they do not happen through contact between muscles or pressure on the muscles, it is more difficult to be aware of the sensation of resonance in their physical movement. You must at times, therefore, exaggerate that movement to get the sensation. Experiment for a moment by speaking the diphthongs made with lip movement 'OH', 'OI' and 'OW'. Speak them slowly with your jaw well open, exaggerating the movement of the lips, making particularly sure that the top lip is moving as vigorously as the bottom one. Take time over the movement so that you feel its weight. After a while you will hear the tone coming to where you are making the movement and that movement contributing to the sound. Then take the tongue diphthongs: with the jaw open move the tongue through the diphthongs 'AY' and 'I' so you feel the weight of the movement. Do this until you feel the sound coming together with the movement as if the movement itself was sending out the sound.

It is essential to the quality of the voice that the tone is placed consistently for both vowels and consonants. The tone should come to where the vowels and consonants are being formed so that the sound and word are together. It is quite common to find that the tone for the consonant is forward and back or medial for the vowel. The adjustment that sometimes has to be made is very subtle and takes time but it is good to work the vowel and consonant exercises together so that they never become separate in feeling and you can continually balance them in relation to each other.

As I have said, vowels and consonants are made with relatively small movements which must, therefore, be defined very particularly. You are also working within a compact space which makes it difficult to separate the relative tensions of the muscles. For example, when making an 'l' the tongue tip has to have tension while the back of the tongue should be quite free, and when making the consonant 'b' the lips need to have pressure yet the back of the throat must be quite relaxed or the tone will be strangled. For 'OO' the lips need tension to round for that sound but if the back of the tongue is tense it will alter the vowel completely. This is why a bone-prop is of such value as it allows you to feel each movement separately. It is essential to keep your head and neck totally free of tension while making these muscles work with great firmness. Initially, when you do the articulation exercises you will find yourself unconsciously pushing with your head as if it were helping to push the sounds out. This, of course, makes the neck tight and closes the throat, tensing the back of the tongue and palate. If this happens it will close off the resonance from the chest and pharynx and the rest of the body and so negate the freedom you could get from the breath.

The energy needed to make words must be specific to the muscles involved: no other effort is needed. Any tension in the neck and throat confuses the clarity. Tension is energy kept back, therefore wasted and irrelevant. All the muscles that are not being used should be relaxed as if doing no work at all. You need to be able to get a sense of the words springing out. Words contain their own energy and you do not need to push them. As soon as you push them you cloud their meaning and reduce their size.

The sound starts with the breath, is resonated, and comes to the word which then sends it out. When the intention, the sound and the word are together you have clarity. When you find this economy of effort in speaking you can stop being emphatic. This is interesting because in an anxiety to convey the meaning you so often rely on emphasis. This is done very often by pushing out the consonants which at once cuts down on the possibilities of length and rhythm in a word. You tend to think that it is only the consonant that you must sharpen. In fact, the energy is in the whole word. If you rely on emphasis to get over your meaning and impinge on the listener, even if not in a crude way, you are unconsciously holding on to the meaning yourself and therefore limiting it. In doing so, you tie your voice down by keeping it only at a logical level. The listener wants to hear what the word contains so that it is allowed to work for him. If you have the confidence to allow the word its full value the meaning is shared and you at once take the pressure off yourself. Firmness without pressure – that is, the right energy – is the balance you are after.

The exercises work at different levels. Practically, they are necessary for clear speech, for projecting that speech and for placing the tone forward in the mouth, so that the muscles themselves and the resonating spaces of the mouth and nose are contributing to the sound as a whole. They are also necessary at another level which is the discovery of the right amount of energy to communicate and the sharing and discovery of meaning.

EXERCISES

These exercises should be done after those for relaxation and breathing so that the awareness of the latter is carried on into these. However, at the beginning do not try to combine the breathing exercises with them as that will confuse the issue and you will not be able to become aware of the separateness of the muscles. The sense of relaxation and freedom in the head, neck and shoulders must be kept throughout. It is essential to start with them absolutely free and in a good position and to check on this frequently during the exercises.

1 **Jaw**
Drop it gently and find its most open and tension-free position. Open and close it several times quite easily, creating no tension. It should not be difficult to open it fairly wide (about two fingers' width is most satisfactory), but if the jaw is stiff then exercise it frequently by doing chewing movements. This can be done at odd moments during the day so it should loosen up quite quickly. It is most important to get it as free as possible without tension.

2 **Tongue-tip**
Insert the bone-prop or, if you are not using one, put one finger on each lip corner to keep the jaw open, comfortable and constant.

a Say: lah

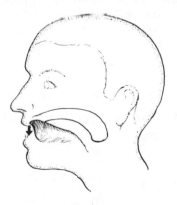

53

Feel the pressure of the tongue tip against the ridge behind the teeth yet not touching the teeth. Keep the tongue there for a moment so you feel its position, then release it into the vowel. Let the 'l' spring easily into the vowel 'AH' which should be open as the vowel in 'last'. The back of the tongue should be free and the throat open and relaxed for the vowel. The tongue-tip should come to rest at the bottom of the mouth behind the teeth. The tension should be specific to the tongue-tip, and the movement should not be jerky. The tongue should spring the vowel out.

Keeping that movement complete, exercise the tongue firmly and rhythmically. Keep the beat the same but increase the number of syllables:

la	lah	lah	lah
lala	lala	lala	lala
lalala	lalala	lalala	lalala

The rhythm should be precise and the movement accurate with the tongue-tip going right down each time. Do not let the tongue slur as you increase the number of syllables.

Repeat this exercise several times with the prop, feeling the precise energy in the tongue tip. Then do it several times without the prop, feeling the tongue-tip working completely on its own with no effort elsewhere. A clean, economical, free sound.

This progression of doing exercises first with and then without the prop, but keeping the precision of movement, should be the same throughout all the exercises.

b With the tip behind the teeth ridge and the sides of the tongue firmly against the top gums say:

tah

Hold the pressure a moment so you feel the contact between the tongue and teeth ridge and notice the explosion of air on the release of the tongue. No breath should escape on the holding of the consonant as that produces a messy sound, but the right amount of air should explode on release, as this is what gives it its bite and carrying power. Test it by putting your hand up in front of your mouth and feeling the air. This also helps you to hear whether it is the right pressure and the right release. It should be firm but not jerky.

Now exercise it, several times with and then without the prop, keeping it absolutely accurate:

tah	tah	tah	tah
tetete	tetete	tetete	tah

c With the position and pressure the same as for 't', say

dah

First of all hold the pressure for a moment so you place the pressure in your mind. You should feel the beginning of the vibration between the tongue and ridge as this is a voiced sound. The vibration should be quite positive as you release it so you will know the sound is placed. Although it is a voiced consonant there will be the smallest fraction of breath escaping to carry the plosion out. This aspiration is necessary to give the sound a certain edge though, of course, almost all the breath is made into sound.

Now exercise it with and without the prop several times, being very conscious of its resonance:

dah   dah   dah   dah
dedede dedede dedede dedede

d With the position of the tongue the same as for 'd', say:

nah

For this consonant, of course, the soft palate is lowered to allow the sound to escape through the nose.

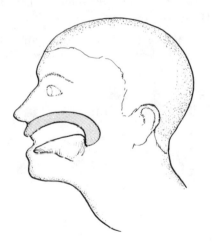

Hold the sound for a moment, feeling the position of the tongue and the vibration on the tongue-tip and resonance in the nose.

Then exercise the tongue several times on that sound, with and without the prop:

nah   nah   nah   nah

nenene   nenene   nenene   nenene

It is important to feel the tongue as muscularly firm as for 'd', otherwise the nasal resonance will continue into the vowel and overlay the tone with nasality. The subsequent vowel must always be released clearly through the mouth and not partially through the nose. (Later exercises for the soft palate will help this.) To get this firmness on 'n' it helps to alternate it with 'd', thus:

dedede   nenene   dedede   nenene

3 **Back of the tongue**

e Exercising the back of the tongue is vital not only for clarity of diction but for the release of the sound as a whole. If the back of the tongue is slack it makes the tone and speech thick and difficult to get forward. This slackness is particularly noticeable in speech that is slightly cockney; the vowels can be standard but if that thickness is there it gives a quality which stamps the speech. Also, these exercises are the only way you can become aware of the soft palate (as unlike the tongue, it is not under direct sensory control), and, therefore, the only way you can free it adequately. If there is tension in the back of the soft palate it affects the tone considerably, putting a metallic nasal skin on it and making it unmalleable. These exercises are important for the sound as a whole.

First of all, press the back of the tongue up against the soft palate which lowers to meet it and notice the pressure. The contact should be firm. Say:

kah

gah

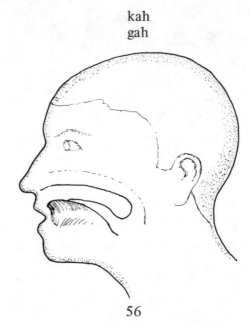

56

If you press the tongue too far up there will be tension and if too far back the sound will be throaty. Try the different positions: press up too much, making tension, then too far back, then feel the tension just right. It helps to judge the sound if you put your hands up a little way in front of the mouth. This also helps you to find the right pressure. Try to get a sense of the consonant hitting the outer air.

Now exercise the tongue:

kekeke   kekeke   kekeke   kah

Feel the breath exploding out.

gegege   gegege   gegege   gah

Feel the vibration between the tongue and the palate with just the slightest aspiration sending the sound out.

Practise both sounds with and without the prop several times. You should get the feeling of the sounds exploding forward, cleanly and effortlessly.

f Because awareness of the palate and back of the tongue is so vital to the sound, take time to do the following exercise, experimenting with the tensions:

Press the tongue hard up against the palate, consciously making tension as for 'ge'. Hold it a moment then release it into the vowel 'er'; you will hear how tight the vowel is. Now press it again firmly but without tension, allowing the back of the palate to come down and meet the tongue. With both sets of muscles firm but free, say 'g' feeling the vibration in both sets of muscles. Then drop the jaw open and say 'AH', feeling the throat completely open and the space behind the tongue resonating the sound:

ge	.... tight	NG	.... tight
ge	.... free	NG	.... free
AH	.... very open	AH	.... open
ge	.... tight	NG	.... tight
ge	.... free	NG	.... free
AY	.... very open	AY	.... open

This is a very useful exercise to use because it is so simple and can be done more or less anywhere and because it is so releasing. Coupled with a gentle nod of the head it is quite excellent.

The Lips

g Press the whole of the lips together so that they cover each other. Feel the pressure and say:

pah

This, of course, is an exaggerated position but is necessary to begin with. Now exercise with a good deal of pressure involving the whole of your lips:

pepepe   pepepe   pepepe   pah

Quite a lot of breath will explode out and it should feel like a cork popping.

h   Holding the lips together for a moment first, feel the possibility of vibration there:

bah

Then exercise the lips:

bebebe   bebebe   bebebe   bah

Do both these exercises several times, first with and then without the prop.

If you are pressing the lips well you will find that they cannot continue for too long or they will begin to go numb. In normal speech you do not use them anything like as fully.

This is one of the best ways to get the sound forward and sense the resonance in the mouth. Notice the vibration on the 'b', though again there is the smallest amount of aspiration to make it carry.

The involvement of the lips in speaking – and I do not mean ultimately moving them a lot, I mean the sense of awareness in them – is directly related to the sense of sharing what you have to say. Immobility of the lips actually gives the impression of reluctance to speak: it is like a curtain hiding the words. The movement is exaggerated in exercise to pinpoint their position in speech.

i   'm' is a nasal consonant so the soft palate is lowered, yet the sound must be muscularly firm and the subsequent vowel clear of nasality:

mah

Hold the sound a moment so you feel the vibration. Then exercise the lips:

mememe   mememe   mememe   mah
mememe   bebebe   mememe   bebebe

The 'm' should be as muscularly firm as the 'b', with a sense of the sound springing out and the vowel clean of nasality. This means that the palate and tongue have to be quite released.

4 Vowel Exercises

a The lips. Exercise rounding the lips from an open position to a
rounded one:

AH   OO

The tongue and palate should be quite free, the lip corners not pulled
back for 'AH', and the movement of the lips very firm.

Do this several times, first with the prop and then without it. Do not
let the lips slur into 'OO'.

Then exercise:

AH   AW   OO

Feel the tone being made on the lips for 'AW' as this is one sound
which is often placed back. Its position is about half-way between
'AH' and 'OO'.

AH   AW   OH   OO

Feel the diphthongal movement of the lips on 'OH' and make sure the
tongue is absolutely free as it can alter that sound.

Feel the precise movement of the lips so each sound is separate and
defined, the tone being sent out by this specific movement. When
the tone is placed specifically the words will have the same specific
quality.

Now put the vowel and consonant together, first with the prop and
then without:

MAH	MAW	MOH	MOO
PAH	PAW	POH	POO
BAH	BAW	BOH	BOO
LAH	LAW	LOH	LOO

Be aware of both the vowel and consonant movement so that the
consonant does not jerk and the vowel is forward.

It is essential that the upper lip is as flexible as the lower. See what
happens when you consciously keep the upper lip immobile. At once
you feel its muscular interrelation with the palate, making the
palate stiff and keeping the placing of the tone back.

b Without the prop so that the jaw moves freely, exaggerate the lip
movements and feel their weight:

OI   OW

For 'OI' feel the first 'AW' sound before it moves to 'i'.

MOI	MOW
POI	POW
BOI	BOW

This is excellent for freeing the lips.

c Now exercise the tongue vowels. Say:

AH   EE

Do this several times, first with the prop and then without. Keeping the soft palate and the back of the tongue completely free, move the tongue frόm the flat position for 'AH' to a highly arched forward position for 'EE'.

Keep the tip of the tongue down behind the bottom teeth, so you feel the blade of the tongue moving quite separately.

d Again with the tip of the tongue still, exercise the blade of the tongue:

AH	AY	EE	
AH	AY	EE	I (as in 'lie')

The sounds 'AY' and 'I' are diphthongal so you feel the blade of the tongue move quite considerably as you say them. Feel the resonance on the tongue for all the vowels: it should be as if the tongue is sending the vowel out.

Do this several times with and without the prop.

e Put the vowels together with the consonant, the consonant firm but not jerky and the vowel retaining that same muscular firmness:

LAH	LAY	LEE	LI
TAH	TAY	TEE	TI
DAH	DAY	DEE	DI

The consonant should assist the vowel forward.

f Without the prop exercise the tongue on the two diphthongs:

AY	IE
LAY	LIE

Feel the movement on the blade of the tongue. This is one of the most freeing exercises for the tone and can be used a lot with the breathing exercises as I have already illustrated.

g Feel the movement of the front part of the blade of the tongue, only for these the tongue starts in a high arched position and goes down:

EAR	AIR
LEAR	LAIR
TEAR	TAIR
DEAR	DAIR

Do this several times with and without the prop.

h   Without the prop, very relaxed and quietly, feel the vibration on the lips, tongue and in the front of the mouth as you say:

> bebebebebebe
> dededededede
> memememememe
> nenenenenene

Use the following voiced continuant consonants for making a steady continued sound:

> v–v–v–v–v–v–v–v–v–v
> z–z–z–z–z–z–z–z–z–z
> th–th–th–th–th–th–th–th–th–th

Use those voiced continuant consonants again in conjunction with vowels to bring the vowels right forward:

VOH	ZOH	THOH	
VAY	ZAY	THAY	etc.

You have now worked on all the sets of muscles involved in making words, felt the energy required, and noticed the extra dimension of resonance they give to the sound. Now try to put this together on a piece of text. Dylan Thomas's *Under Milk Wood* is first-rate for the purpose. Any part of it will do, but here I have included a short piece spoken by the First Voice. The sense is not complicated; it is very physical language and so reinforces the muscularity you have been working at. In other words, you do not feel ridiculous exaggerating the muscular movement when doing it as you might with more sober text, for it is extravagant anyway. Do, however, resist the temptation of doing it in a Welsh accent as this will not help your purpose!

To begin with, use it as an exercise, doing it in these stages:

i   With the bone-prop, slowly and noticing the complete movement of each vowel and consonant and how one moves into the other. There are, of course, sounds which are not possible to make completely with the prop — those requiring a closed jaw such as 's', 'z', 'CH' and 'dg', or 'th', 'f' and 'v' when the prop actually obstructs the formation. Otherwise, try to make it as clear as possible. Be

61

particularly accurate in finishing off the final consonants such as
'l' and the voiced 's' sounds as on 'girls', 'mothers', and so on.

ii   Without the prop, but slowly, making all the muscular
movement complete. Allow the jaw to be very free (exaggerate the
opening to begin with) but, as you go on, cut it down to a normal
opening.

iii   Cup your hands round your mouth under your nose so that they
act as a megaphone, and speak part of the text. The hands round your
mouth add a certain resonance and therefore encourage your own.
This pinpoints where the sound should be placed. When you take
your hands away you will notice the difference in sound. This is most
valuable to do on any piece of text.

iv   Speak the piece without exaggeration, beginning to focus on
the meaning yet keeping the energy in the vowels and consonants.
Begin to join the two together so that it acts as a bridge between the
physical and mental processes. When you are ready, join it up with
the breathing exercise.

This is a good progression to do on any piece of text.

From *UNDER MILK WOOD*

And the shrill girls giggle and master around him and squeal as they
clutch and thrash, and he blubbers away downhill with his patched
pants falling, and his tear-splashed blush burns all the way as the
triumphant bird-like sisters scream with buttons in their claws and
the bully brothers hoot after him his little nickname and his mother's
shame and his father's wickedness with the loose wild barefoot women
of the hovels of the hills. It all means nothing at all, and, howling for
his milky mum, for her cawl and buttermilk and cowbreath and
welshcakes and the fat birth-smelling bed and moonlit kitchen of her
arms, he'll never forget as he paddles blind home through the weeping
end of the world. Then his tormentors tussle and run to the Cockle
Street sweet-shop, their pennies sticky as honey, to buy from Miss
Myfanwy Price, who is cocky and neat as a puff-bosomed robin and
her small round buttocks tight as ticks, gobstoppers big as wens that
rainbow as you suck, brandyballs, winegums, hundreds and thousands,
liquorice sweet as sick, nougat to tug and ribbon out like another red
rubbery tongue, gum to glue in girls' curls, crimson coughdrops to
spit blood, ice-cream cornets, dandelion-and-burdock, raspberry and
cherryade, pop goes the weasel and the wind.

Dylan Thomas

This is an extraordinarily good piece of text to use as, indeed, is any of *Under Milk Wood* for it clarifies something of the relation between the meaning of words and their physical make-up: without having to explain it, you feel the relation as you make the sounds. As I said in the first chapter, physiological changes take place when strong feelings are involved. In this particular passage you are told of the feeling of a child's shame. Everyone can recognise these sensations of shame, and the physical meaning of 'blubbers away', 'tear-splashed blush burns all the way', 'mother's shame' and 'moonlit kitchen of her arms' is contained in the physical weight and making of those words. Somewhere the weight of both is interrelated.

I would like to be a little more specific about the exact shaping of the vowels and the relation of vowel and consonant. This, of course, is particularly valuable for the placing of the tone.

Quietly and easily go through the following progressions of vowels, first with and then without the prop:

1

OO	oo	OH
(lose)	(look)	(load)

Feel the position for each precisely. The back of the tongue should be quite free and open so there is no slight 'er' quality to 'OO'. The lips should not slur into the sound, and their movement must be firm. 'oo' is short but has a specific lip rounding, though not so much as 'OO'. 'OH' starts with the lips hardly rounded and glides towards 'oo'. The tone should be absolutely with the movement. As you become familiar with the progression say it quicker but keep precise. The movement between each is quite small.

Then put consonants in front:

LOO	Loo	LOH
POO	Poo	POH
BOO	Boo	BOH
MOO	Moo	MOH

2 Do the same with:

AW	o	OW
(fork)	(fox)	(fowl)

The jaw should feel long for 'AW' and the sound particularly forward on the lips, as this is a vowel that tends to get placed back as the back of the tongue is raised a little for it, and sometimes the sound stays with the tongue. Also, make sure 'o' is placed forward on the lips as there is little rounding for it. 'OW' starts with the lips open on a sound somewhere between 'AH' and 'u', and rounds to 'oo', but be sure it is placed with the movement of the lips. The weight of the vowel is on the first sound.

Now put consonants in front:

LAW	Lo	LOW
PAW	Po	POW
BAW	Bo	BOW
MAW	Mo	MOW

3 Now say:

OI

This starts with a very firm 'AW' and ends with the lips open, moving to the tongue position of 'i'. Use this in conjunction with the consonants as above.

4 For the tongue vowels try the following progression of vowels, starting with the tongue flat for 'AH' with the lip corners relaxed and not pulled back at all. Gradually raise the front part of the blade of the tongue until it is arching quite high for 'EE'. Keep the tip of the tongue quite steady behind the lower teeth for the exercise. It is the front part of the blade that should move, the back of the tongue being as relaxed as possible with the throat open. The movement between each vowel is quite slight and should be felt very precisely, for it is the precise awareness of the placing of the tongue which bears directly on the definition of the vowels and consequently on the placing of the tone. The tone should come to where the vowel is being made.

With and without the bone-prop, say:

AH – u – ER – a – e
(bark) (bud) (bird) (bad) (bed)

– AY – i – EE – I
(bake) (bid) (bead) (buy)

'AY' starts with the tongue at an open 'e' position and glides towards the sound 'i'. 'I' starts with the tongue in the position somewhere between 'AH' and 'u' (as with 'OW') and also glides towards 'i'. With both 'AY' and 'I' it is the first sound that holds the weight of the vowel and the tongue only glides towards 'i' but does not dwell on the latter sound. This is most important, because if you say the latter sound fully it will give a cockney sound to the speech.

These vowels are particularly useful for placing the tone as you feel the movement of the tongue when saying them. It makes the tongue much more subtle and mobile, and the muscularity contains its own resonance. You can feel the vibrations on the tongue when singing or speaking them fully, and you can feel the tongue sending out the tone.

These last exercises require time, but it is important that the vowels are experienced separately and their position understood because of the clarity the right placing gives to the speech. Obviously, in normal speech they can never be so open because they are always in context of a word, so that they are always coming to or going from a consonant which modifies their position. In any case, it would be false to have them so open. The separate experience of them is essential so that the comparable freedom and placing carries over into normal speech.

Try the same progression of the tongue vowels with a consonant preceding each one. Do this once or twice with the prop, but mainly without it to allow the jaw to open freely for each vowel. Be aware of the friction and vibration on the consonant smoothly going into the placing of the vowel. Do not hurry the movement and feel the weight of each sound:

LAH	Lu	LER	La	Le	LAY	Li	LEE	LI
TAH	Tu	TER	Ta	Te	TAY	Ti	TEE	TI
DAH	Du	DER	Da	De	DAY	Di	DEE	DI
NAH	Nu	NER	Na	Ne	NAY	Ni	NEE	NI
PAH	Pu	PER	Pa	Pe	PAY	Pi	PEE	PI
BAH	Bu	BER	Ba	Be	BAY	Bi	BEE	BI
MAH	Mu	MER	Ma	Me	MAY	Mi	MEE	MI
KAH	Ku	KER	Ka	Ke	KAY	Ki	KEE	KI
GAH	Gu	GER	Ga	Ge	GAY	Gi	GEE	GI
VAH	Vu	VER	Va	Ve	VAY	Vi	VEE	VI
ZAH	Zu	ZER	Za	Ze	ZAY	Zi	ZEE	ZI
THAH	Thu	THER	Tha	The	THAY	Thi	THEE	THI

Without tension or pushing, be aware of the consonant sending the vowel out, and the vowel containing its own resonance. Each sound has its own energy, and this awareness is something you need to remember, for it is the energy that projects the word physically and without effort.

In order to hear exactly what difference the placing of these vowels makes to the tone, try doing them once with the jaw almost closed so that the tongue can make little movement. You will be able to make the vowels recognizable, but you will hear that the tone stays in the back of the mouth. The back of the tongue is particularly tense because it is having to make the vowels in a very constricted way, and the vowels themselves have no definition. They are also liable to be nasal, as there is not a free enough passage through the mouth. Repeat the progression of vowels with the throat open, the jaw free allowing the tongue space to form the sounds. You can immediately draw your own conclusions. Of course, you were exaggerating the closed position of the jaw and so sending the vowels right back, but in fact most people have limited vowel definition to some degree. The essential thing to realise is that even a slight lack of freedom in the jaw, lips and tongue restricts the sound and limits what you can do with the voice. It limits the energy of the voice.

Now to find the specific energy in the consonants. Consonants at the beginning of words carry more impulse than those at the end, that is to say they require slightly more breath. Also you must be aware of the different sensation of the breathed consonant and the voiced one.

Take the tongue consonants with this sequence of vowels:

TOO	TOH	TAW	TAH	TAY	TEE
DOO	DOH	DAW	DAH	DAY	DEE
NOO	NOH	NAW	NAH	NAY	NEE

Feel the right pressure of the tongue against the teeth ridge that we found earlier, let the jaw be open for the vowel. With the 't' you will hear a small explosion of breath immediately after you release the consonant. With 'd' you will feel vibration between the tip of tongue and the teeth ridge and just the smallest amount of breath on its release. It is this small release of air on the consonant that gives the speech its bite and carries the sound out. With 'n', the back of the palate is lowered allowing the sound to be resonated in the nose. This nasal resonance is valuable to the sound, though the vowel must be placed precisely in the mouth. Take time to feel this balance of vowel and consonant.

Do the same with the lip consonants:

POO	POH	PAW	PAH	PAY	PEE
BOO	BOH	BAW	BAH	BAY	BEE
MOO	MOH	MAW	MAH	MAY	MEE

There is the explosion of breath directly after you release the 'p'. There is friction on the 'b' as you hold it, and a smaller explosion of air as you release it into the vowel. 'm' is resonated in the nose and adds to the vocal resonance, yet, as you release it into the vowel the tone must go to the placing of the vowel.

Similarly with the back of the tongue. Get the right pressure of the tongue on the soft palate and let the sound explode forward:

KOO	KOH	KAW	KAH	KAY	KEE
GOO	GOH	GAW	GAH	GAY	GEE

Feel the breath on the 'k' and the vibration on the 'g'.

Now take the continuant consonants, alternating between breathed and voiced:

FOO	FOH	FAW	FAH	FAY	FEE
VOO	VOH	VAW	VAH	VAY	VEE
SOO	SOH	SAW	SAH	SAY	SEE
ZOO	ZOH	ZAW	ZAH	ZAY	ZEE

THOO (breathed as in 'thin')

THOH	THAW	THAH	THAY	THEE

THOO (voiced as in 'this')

THOH	THAW	THAH	THAY	THEE

Lengthen these consonants slightly so that you feel the breath and the vibration carrying the sound out.

Now put the consonant at the end of the vowel. You will find that they do not have the same amount of breath impulse, but they take fractionally longer to say, but they should be as positive in their contribution to the sound.

OOT	OHT	AWT	AHT	AYT	EET
OOD	OHD	AWD	AHD	AYD	EED
OON	OHN	AWN	AHN	AYN	EEN
OOP	OHP	AWP	AHP	AYP	EEP
OOB	OHB	AWB	AHB	AYB	EEB
OOM	OHM	AWM	AHM	AYM	EEM
OOK	OHK	AWK	AHK	AYK	EEK
OOG	OHG	AWG	AHG	AYG	EEG
OOF	OHF	AWF	AHF	AYF	EEF
OOV	OHV	AWV	AHV	AYV	EEV
OOS	OHS	AWS	AHS	AYS	EES
OOZ	OHZ	AWZ	AHZ	AYZ	EEZ

OOTH (breathed)

OHTH	AWTH	AHTH	AYTH	EETH

OOTH (voiced)

OHTH	AWTH	AHTH	AYTH	EETH

This also helps to make the vowels smooth and full.

There is a difference in the length of a consonant at the end of a word or syllable, according to whether it is a breathed or voiced or continuant consonant, and this difference in length affects the length of the vowel. A voiced consonant takes longer to say than a breathed one. Thus, 'd' takes longer than 't', 'g' takes longer than 'k', and 'b' takes longer than 'p'. Similarly with 'z' and 's', 'v' and 'f', and the voiced and unvoiced 'th'. You will notice the different lengths in the following sequence of words:

sat — sad
rate — raid
feet — feed

A continuant consonant also takes longer than an explosive consonant, so that 'v' takes longer than 'd', and so on, as in the next sequence:

leek — leaf
lead — leave
fit — fill
caught — call
lad — lamb

Again, a combination of consonants takes even longer:

Heart — hard — harm — harms
hat — had — hand — hands
leak — leaf — lead — leads — leave — leaves
set — said — self — selves
rate — raid — rain — range — ranged
girth — gird — girl — girls

The combinations are limitless, and it is quite fascinating to notice the relative quantity of vowels and consonants that there are in a piece of text. It is all part of the particular measure of the words chosen and therefore of the meaning.

Now to make the consonants absolutely clear. Go through the following sequence of vowels and consonants, first with the prop and then without, feeling the complete muscular movement for each consonant. For instance, with 'OOKT' or 'OOGD' you feel the complete movement of the back and front of the tongue separating those consonants more than you would do in normal speech.

OOKT	OHKT	AWKT	AHKT	AYKT	EEKT
OOGD	OHGD	AWGD	AHGD	AYGD	EEGD
OOPT	OHPT	AWPT	AHPT	AYPT	EEPT
OOBD	OHBD	AWBD	AHBD	AYBD	EEBD
OOMD	OHMD	AWMD	AHMD	AYMD	EEMD
OOLT	OHLT	AWLT	AHLT	AYLT	EELT
OOLD	OHLD	AWLD	AHLD	AYLD	EELD
OOLZ	OHLZ	AWLZ	AHLZ	AYLZ	EELZ

Take the following without the prop, as it is not possible to make 's', 'z', 'f', 'v', 'th' satisfactorily with it. Allow the jaw to open as much as possible for this is also excellent as a jaw exercise, as the vowels must be free to form properly.

OOTHT	OHTHT	AWTHT	AHTHT	AYTHT	EETHT
OOTHD	OHTHD	AWTHD	AHTHD	AYTHD	EETHD
OOTHZ	OHTHZ	AWTHZ	AHTHZ	AYTHZ	EETHZ
OOST	OHST	AWST	AHST	AYST	EEST
OOSTS	OHSTS	AWSTS	AHSTS	AYSTS	EESTS
OOZD	OHZD	AWZD	AHZD	AYZD	EEZD
OOFT	OHFT	AWFT	AHFT	AYFT	EEFT
OOFTS	OHFTS	AWFTS	AHFTS	AYFTS	EEFTS
OOVD	OHVD	AWVD	AHVD	AYVD	EEVD
OOKST	OHKST	AWKST	AHKST	AYKST	EEKST
OOTTH	OHTTH	AWTTH	AHTTH	AYTTH	EETTH

This series of vowel sounds combined with any difficult consonant combinations should answer any individual problems of consonant agility.

With this added awareness of the length and placing of vowels, and with the muscularity and quantity of consonants, go back over the piece of Dylan Thomas text that you tried earlier. Take the first sentence and speak only the vowels. Be very conscious of the placing of each one, however short it is. Then do exactly the same with the consonants — isolate and speak each consonant or combination of consonants, feeling all their movement and length. Then speak the sentence quite normally, being aware of the movement of vowel into consonant and the precise pattern they make.

Finally, speak it quite normally, concentrating on the meaning. You will find that the meaning itself opens out enormously because of your awareness of the weight of the words. The hurt described is directly related to the physical making of the words. You can experiment like this with the Milton and the Shakespeare texts which I have already given. Hear the difference in quantity in the lines, and therefore the different movement in them. The different weight in words contains much of the meaning, and awareness of this does a lot of the work for you.

Now a word about accents. It is always difficult dealing with an accent as you may feel that if you speak differently you are in some way betraying your background, or at any rate being false to yourself. I think, also, that there is a deep-rooted feeling that a standard accent is to some degree effeminate, and therefore to remove the accent takes away a certain virility in the speech. This is why a man may find it more difficult to deal with than a woman. Class consciousness goes deeper than we care to admit, even though a standard accent is no longer so defined or confining. It is interesting to notice that it is beginning to be fashionable to speak 'off', though I think this is a superficial thing which does not go against what I have already said. However, if the balance of the accent is over the edge, it limits the parts you can play and the sounds you can make.

If, however, you concentrate on getting the right muscularity and placing of the vowels and consonants and not on correcting 'wrong' ones, you will find you will keep your individuality and at the same time extend the voice to make it able to deal with all kinds of text. The exercises already given, particularly the vowel ones, should answer the problems. Medial vowels are particular to London speech, that is speech that has a cockney flavour but is not actually cockney. This speech often has a nasal quality to it, which is the result of a constricted jaw which does not allow for the full movement of the lips and tongue. This is not restricted to cockney speech, for certain upper class or 'Kensington' accents have the same quality though the choice of vowels, and so the associations, are different. A strong Australian accent is an extreme example of constricted jaw movement affecting the muscular movement of the lips, especially the upper one, and consequently the back of the palate. With this accent all the vowel sounds take place in the middle to back of the mouth, and the back of the tongue has to work particularly hard to define the vowels at all.

It is then the balance of vowels you must concentrate on and the complete movements of the consonants. However, there are four other points to be looked at:

1 *Final 'l' sounds.*   To make 'l' the tongue tip is pressed against the teeth ridge and the sides of the tongue are lowered so that the sound can escape through the spaces on each side of it. However, the back of the tongue alters its position according to whether the 'l' is at the beginning of a word or syllable or at the end. Speak the following sequence of words noticing the position of the back of the tongue for 'l':

leaf – loom – eel – cool – able

The position of the back of the tongue is high for the 'l' at the beginning of words and gradually lowers throughout the sequence. It is also affected by the vowel. Now there is usually no problem with 'l' at the beginning of words – the light 'l' as we call it – but final or dark 'l's can be very unclear. First of all they take time to say and secondly, because the back of the tongue is lower, very often the pressure on the tip is relaxed. So, for final 'l's feel the tip pressed against the teeth ridge, but allow the back to be quite free. Try these words:

feel – field
fill – filled – fills
fail – failed
sell – sells
girl – girls

1 *The curve in the small of the back resulting in bad posture.*

2 *Cicely Berry with actress Lynn Dearth showing the back long and straight and the head lengthening out of the back.*

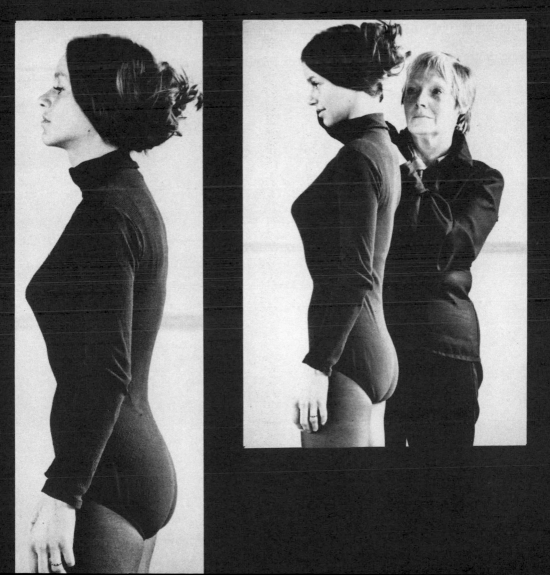

3 Free position on the floor. The back is flat and spread and the knees crooked up.

4 The neck and shoulders are in a tense position so that the neck resonator is not open and free.

5 *Hands on the ribs at the side in a good breathing position. The rest of the body is relaxed.*

6 *Cicely's hands on the ribs at the back showing Lynn where the most rib movement can take place.*

7 *Hands stretched up above the head ready to swing down.*

gnarl — gnarled
fall — falls
foal — fold
cool — cooled

You see that it takes a certain time to make these final 'l's satisfactorily. After the 'EE' vowel there is almost another short 'er'
vowel while the tongue makes its adjustment. It is most important
to allow for this.

2 *Final 'i' vowel sounds.*   These occur at the end of words such as
'quickly', 'quietly', 'possibility', 'city', and so on. These final 'i'
sounds often get lengthened into an 'EE' quality and, in fact they
are always extremely short, as in the word 'vivid'. The best thing to
do is to make lists of words which include this sound and practise
the sound so that you create a new habit.

3 *Syllabic consonants.*   These are consonants which take the
weight of a syllable *without* a vowel. For instance, in the words
'bottle', 'cattle', 'settle', the 'l' sound is a complete syllable. The
mechanism is that you press the tongue up high all the way round
as for 't' and you lower the sides of the tongue into the 'l' position
without making a vowel to bridge the gap. In cockney speech very
often a glottal stop is substituted for the 't' sound or the 't' is not
made completely. When trying to correct it, a small 'er' vowel is
often put in between the two consonants. Neither is right. Practise
by making a list of words which have the same sequence, feeling
the tongue-tip pressed firmly against the teeth ridge for the 't' and
staying there while lowering the sides to form 'l'. The same
principle applies to syllabic 'n' sounds as in 'curtain' and 'cotton'.
The tongue-tip is up for 't' and remains firm while the back of the
palate is lowered to allow it to move into 'n'.

4   Do not be over careful when the same sound ends one word and
begins the next, as in 'want to', or 'could do'. You do not make the
't' or the 'd' sound fully both times, you merely hold on to it longer
to allow for the timing of two sounds.

5 *Nasal vowels.* First get the back of the palate free by exercising:
                kekeke . . . .then AH very open.
                gegege . . . .then AY very open.

Keep that freedom there and take the nasal consonants 'm' and
'n' in conjunction with the vowels, first separating them and then
running them together.

Be aware of the placing of the consonant in the nose, yet allow the
vowel to open through the mouth. Practise with words such as 'moon',
'morning', and so on, slowly to begin with until you get the feeling
of the vowel always being placed in the mouth. It sometimes helps to

71

get a yawning feeling on the vowel.

6 *Devoiced consonants.* The unvoiced consonants such as 's', 'f', 't',
'p', and so on, give sharpness to the speech. But it is very important
that all voiced consonants are properly vibrated, particularly final
ones because they add resonance to the voice. All final 's' sounds
after voiced consonants should be said as 'z'. It is useful to pair the
consonants, the unvoiced with the voiced, and take time to get full
vibration on the latter.

$$p - b$$
$$t - d$$
$$k - g$$
$$s - z$$
$$f - v$$
$$th - th \text{ voiced}$$

The last exercises are particularly valuable for feeling the resonance
in the head.

The next step is to use this extra awareness on material which
demands agility and clarity. I have found great value in taking pieces
of text like the following Dryden and Sitwell poems which are very
rhythmical, and using the rhythm to move to. Take a part of one
of the poems, a few lines to begin with, and repeat them exaggerating
the muscular movement of the words until you know them. Say the
lines in strict time, slowly to begin with and getting quicker as it
becomes easier, and begin to dance to that rhythm. Let the rhythm
of the words give you a freedom of movement, so that you dance
quite vigorously, feeling the movement in the whole of your body,
yet be precise in that movement. You need a certain amount of
space for this, but go on dancing until you feel a buoyancy in the
words and the movement. Keep the diction precise. After a few
minutes you will find that, providing you keep the time in the
movement, you will be able to find all sorts of changes of rhythm in
the words: syncopating them, lengthening them, getting surprising
inflections, and the voice itself will be liberated. When you feel you
have investigated the rhythm, stand still and say the lines. All the
poems in Edith Sitwell's *Facade Suite* are excellent for this purpose,
and they depend on an extraordinary awareness of sound. The
Dryden poem here is different in that it has a logical progression.
When you say it:
  i.   Move in rhythm.
  ii. Keep the timing strict.
  iii. Keep the words sharp as the wit is in the words.
  iv. Tell the story.
In this poem you learn a lot about words doing their own work.

SCOTCH RHAPSODY

'Do not take a bath in Jordan,
Gordon,
On the holy Sabbath, on the peaceful day!'
Said the huntsman, playing on his old bagpipe,
Boring to death the pheasant and the snipe —
Boring the ptarmigan and grouse for fun —
Boring them worse than a nine-bore gun.
Till the flaxen leaves where the prunes are ripe
Heard the tartan wind a-droning in the pipe,
And they heard MacPherson say:
'Where do the waves go? What hotels
Hide their bustles and their gay ombrelles?
And would there be room? — Would there be *room*?
Would there be room for me?'
There is a hotel at Ostend
Cold as the wind, without an end,
Haunted by ghostly poor relations
Of Bostonian conversations
(Bagpipes rotting through the walls).
And there the pearl-ropes fall like shawls
With a noise like marine waterfalls.
And 'Another little drink wouldn't do us any harm'
Pierces through the Sabbatical calm.
And that is the place for me!
So do not take a bath in Jordan,
Gordon,
On the holy Sabbath, on the peaceful day —
Or you'll never go to heaven, Gordon MacPherson,
And speaking purely as a private person
That is the place — *that* is the place — that is the *place*
for me!

Edith Sitwell

SONG

Sylvia the Fair, in the bloom of Fifteen
Felt an innocent warmth, as she lay on the green;
She had heard of a pleasure, and something she guessed
By the towzing and tumbling and touching her Breast:
She saw the men eager, but was at a loss,
What they meant by their sighing and kissing so close;
      By their praying and whining,
      And clasping and twining,
      And panting and wishing,
      And sighing and kissing,
      And sighing and kissing so close.

Ah she cry'd, ah for a languishing Maid
In a Country of Christians to die without aid;
Not a Whig, or a Tory, or Trimmer at least,
Or a Protestant Parson or Catholick Priest,
To instruct a young Virgin that is at a loss
What they meant by their sighing and kissing so close:
      By their praying and whining,
      And clasping and twining,
      And panting and wishing,
      And sighing and kissing,
      And sighing and kissing so close.

Cupid in Shape of a Swayn did appear,
He saw the sad wound, and in pity drew near,
Then showed her his Arrow, and bid her not fear,
For the pain was no more than a Maiden may bear;
When the balm was infused, she was not at a loss
What they meant by their sighing and kissing so close,
      By their praying and whining,
      And clasping and twining,
      And panting and wishing,
      And sighing and kissing,
      And sighing and kissing so close.

John Dryden

The following lyric by Robert Herrick is quite marvellous for hearing the balance of vowels and consonants and the music they have in themselves. Go through a couple of verses very quietly, first isolating the vowels and then the consonants. Then speak it quietly being aware of the precision of each syllable. Then say it with the meaning, hearing the rhythm. Notice how each line has precisely the same number of syllables, yet the movement in each line is different. The sound contains a dimension of the meaning.

TO ANTHEA, WHO MAY COMMAND HIM ANYTHING

Bid me to live, and I will live
    Thy Protestant to be;
Or bid me love, and I will give
    A loving heart to thee.

A heart as soft, a heart as kind,
    A heart as sound and free
As in the whole world thou canst find,
    That heart I'll give to thee.

Bid that heart stay, and it will stay
    To honour thy decree:
Or bid it languish quite away,
    And't shall do so for thee.

Bid me to weep, and I will weep
    While I have eyes to see:
And, having none, yet will I keep
    A heart to weep for thee.

Bid me despair, and I'll despair
    Under that Cypress-tree:
Or bid me die, and I will dare
    E'en death to die for thee.

Thou art my life, my love, my heart,
    The very eyes of me:
And hast command of every part
    To live and die for thee.

                            Robert Herrick

4 The Whole Voice

I have dealt with the main technical means to get the voice working with freedom and agility by separately working on the mechanics of breathing and speaking. It is important now to find ways of putting it all together and getting the voice working as a whole — of expanding it in order to find all its range and texture.

First I think it is important to be quite clear that the exercises have nothing to do with making you technically more accomplished. They are for the purpose of freeing the voice so that it is able to respond to the instinct of the moment. For however openly you are working, if the voice has not the breadth and experience of resonance and ways of making sound its response will be limited. It can only respond to the extent that it is capable of making sound.

Everyone will be at different stages with the exercises but this does not matter for there is no competition. Some will need particular concentration on the competence and freedom of the speech or will need to open up resonance and depth. Others will find the exercises necessary to keep them agile and open. It is interesting to see that they have their purpose at every level. It is also vitally important that when you do the exercises you notice what is happening. That is to say, they should never be done automatically: there must always be some part of yourself noticing what happens and therefore developing your awareness.

As you do the exercises you will find that where you are technically at fault will have something to do with your own motive being out of balance. This is where the self-awareness and the noticing matters. Here are some examples:

1 You will find that if the diction is not quite clear, physically it can be put right with exercise. But it also has something to do with not being quite precise in thought or not carrying the thought through into the word. It may also have something to do with generalised emotion.

2 Over-explosive consonants and over-emphatic speech has something to do with lack of trust in your own ability to communicate, so you push the sense out and explain. As soon as you are over-emphatic you stop the possibilities of the sense.

3 Losing the ends of words can be put right technically, but it is also tied up with not thinking through to the end of a thought — that is, rushing from one thought to another without giving it time to touch down. Again this is lack of trust.

4 A stiff jaw and lack of mobility in the lips is partly habit and use but it can also be to do with reluctance to communicate.

5 Clipped vowels are partly due to the fact that few people actually hear the music in vowels or hear their infinite variety of length. It is also to do with not committing yourself fully to the feeling and being afraid of showing emotion. This keeps text at a down to earth logical level where sometimes it may need to sing.

6 Breathiness and devoicing of voiced consonants means that you are letting all the breath go in a rush, which arises from anxiety to please. One must keep a reserve of strength because you can only afford to be vulnerable for moments.

7 Too much resonance, overbalance of resonance to word and an emotional quality, means that in some way you are more involved with a general emotional quality than with the organic reason for that emotion.

Self-diagnosis is, therefore, important. You must listen to criticism and analyse it because you do need a reliable outside ear telling you from time to time exactly what you are communicating. Curiously enough, you usually know what criticism is constructive and what you can discard. Gradually you come to a more accurate judgment of yourself.

The time you spend on exercises will vary tremendously with the individual, as will the kind of progression you make for yourself. There is no method, simply an attitude to voice which comes out of a fuller understanding of its workings. Obviously, the first need is to get to a point where the exercises can be done accurately and with ease; but I do think it is important at whatever stage you are at, that you do not stick just to exercises for this is stilting. The voice will never be as good in exercise as it will be when you have done the exercises, forgotten them, and are using the voice imaginatively. From the very beginning you must start to use the voice on material that will stretch it, material that can be used over and over again because it is possible to get different things out of it each time. I have included texts here to be used for just this purpose. You will find that they all require particular skill and, of course, they will lead you on to find more things for yourself.

It is the progression into the passages that is important, for speaking them must come out of the freedom you have found in the breathing and muscularity exercises. You must take that awareness into the speaking so that as you speak them the emphasis gradually shifts from technical ability into the interpretation of the sense. You must use whatever works for you in breathing and singing until you get the sound free.

In practice you must observe this progression:

1 Consciously put the breathing into practice on a part of the text — that is, open up the ribs and get the sound rooted to the

diaphragm. You cannot remind yourself too often that it is only when you feel the breath touching down and the sound springing from it that the voice will be of your own authorship.

2 Speak a part of the text exaggerating the muscular movement of the vowels and the consonants, and the moving from one sound to another. This can be done with the prop or without it but moving the jaw very freely.

3 It is of immense value to sing parts of these texts either on the same note, like a chant, or making your own tune so it sounds like a recitative. Allow the sense to dictate the singing phrases you use but let the phrases extend and elongate so that you feel the need to use plenty of breath. Continue by speaking the text, still allowing the phrases to extend and using a good breadth of range; you will feel a good deal of power and freedom after this. It also makes you very aware of rhythm changes in the text.

4 Hum on various notes, high, middle and low, first putting your hands on your head to encourage and feel the resonance in the bones of the head, then covering your face with your hands to encourage and feel the resonance in the sinuses and the bones of the face. Take time over this, making sure the breath is behind the note. You can move about and jog up and down while doing so. Then test the forward resonance by making the continuant voiced consonants 'V', 'Z' and 'TH' and holding on to them. Continue by speaking a piece of text feeling these resonances, but always be sure the resonance collects on the word so that the head resonance does not overbalance it.

5 With plenty of breath backing the sound speak the text loudly, pitching part of it right up out of your normal speaking range. Make absolutely sure that the sound is still rooted. Key it high and then gradually let it come down to your normal key so that you resolve your inflections on your normal base note, but continue to incorporate the high notes. Most people are very dull in the amount of range they use, partly because of a feeling that it is false to use too much (a question of habit and appropriateness) and perhaps because they feel that the upper notes are not as good. It is interesting to listen to someone with a really good, strong, low voice who is free enough to use high notes within the context of what he is saying. Also, doing this exercise has a very freeing effect when you come to use your normal middle range. I think it is a misconception that a low voice is necessarily more interesting. When you listen to people talking who are involved with what they are saying you notice what extraordinary inflections they use which seem quite appropriate. When you come to the printed text this freedom of range goes. You need, therefore, to get to the point where you feel you can respond with any note and a light on anything. Really use this exercise to

experiment with range and to become familiar with more notes.

6 Notice the sweep in your inflections and make sure that they are resolved satisfactorily. Sometimes people have what we call minor tone — that is, they do not take the whole sweep of an inflection and somehow cut its curve, resolving it in half tones. This is something which is very difficult to be aware of oneself and a tape recorder is often useful to work with. I do not believe in working with tapes unless it is absolutely necessary as, on the whole, they make you self-conscious in the wrong way. But when it is a question of ear and the judgment of particular sounds, as with accents or resolving inflections, then they are unquestionably useful. They enable you to make the adjustment between what you hear in your head and what is actually coming out and recognise the differences between the two. For minor tone it is helpful to use narrative material, concentrating on telling a story. This kind of use is not an actor's use but does help you to experience greater freedom of pitch.

I have always felt that poetry is quite the best material to use because the demands it makes are very particular and quite subtle, yet its extravagance encourages you to do extravagant things which are not untrue. This has nothing to do with what kind of acting you want to do; it is not just for the person who wants to do mainly classical acting but for those using all kinds of text. The point is, you find inflections happen which if they had been calculated would seem false, but which if they spring from the stimulation of a text are quite true. Speeches from plays are not always helpful as they cannot be done without reference to character and interpretation and other issues than voice immediately become important. It is the form in poetry that gives you the freedom to be extravagant and to respond in surprising ways: it is useful to work within the discipline of its framework. There is, of course, some splendid prose material, such as the sermons of John Donne, passages from James Joyce and passages of oratory. However, there is something limiting in them. Poetry is totally direct speech and absolutely open to the person who is speaking.

The other essential thing about it is that it increases your awareness of rhythms, lengths of words, finding ways of suspending rhythm while the sense goes on so that you learn to keep a drive through a passage without rushing. It makes you more aware of major and minor inflections, and it teaches you how to give the listener the logical footholds which he needs to cling on to for his understanding, while allowing heightened language to be enjoyed — that is, interweaving the logical with the lyrical. When experimenting with the two poems *Sylvia the Fair* and *Scotch Rhapsody* the fact

79

that you had to keep strict time because of the dance movement made you vocally more malleable: it helps the manipulation of the voice.

Experiment with these passages as boldly as you can, first as an extension to the exercises but always getting around to speaking them with no exaggeration and interpreting them at the stage of understanding you have reached with them. The freedom will be there. Each passage required particular things from the voice, so I have included some notes on each passage as a guide to this.

1 *The Ode to the West Wind.* This is marvellous because it has tremendous breadth of sound and really long phrases. It should not be hurried as you will hear that its weight lies in the quantity of sound in each word — that is, the vowels are, in the main, long and open as in 'wild', 'being', 'grave', 'airy', 'destroyer', and so on. There are a lot of voiced continuant consonants used for their length, such as 'leaves', 'grave', 'azure', 'angels', 'cleave themselves into chasms', 'oozy woods', and so on. As you see, there is often more than one continuant consonant to a syllable and this, quite literally, takes more time to speak and therefore requires more breath. Because the words themselves refer to life-giving properties — 'breath', 'being', 'impulse', 'be thou, Spirit fierce, My Spirit' — they need the particular rooted quality that you want to get from the breath. It should not be hurried for its value is in the continuous resonant sound it requires, and within each stanza there is a different movement and a different key. In the first stanza the wind is related to the earth and the seeds of the earth. The second stanza explores its effect on the clouds and the sky: it is the moving force of the element of air. The third stanza relates the wind to the sea. In the fourth stanza Shelley brings these ideas together and begins to relate himself to the wind and in the fifth he identifies himself and his own spirit with the wind. You can see that there is tremendous vocal scope in its variety of rhythm and texture, for each image has breadth and yet is quite personal and special to Shelley so that you have to find the reality of each image. This poem is excellent for stretching the breathing and for finding a gradual mounting drive and strength without losing particularness and keeping quite free.

2 The opening passage of *Under Milk Wood.* It is fairly obvious what is needed here. The language is muscular and full of imagery; there is warmth and irony in the way Thomas turns the words to give his personal impression of a small Welsh town where even the wind is musical. It needs alertness to the image for almost every word contains a picture. Do not be tempted to speak it with a Welsh accent. Although ultimately it needs that particular manipulation of language, it would not answer the particular purpose for which it is there. In any case, you will be influenced by its musicality. Be as

precise as you can with the words for then the incredible humour will come over.

3 Extract from *Epithalamion*. This requires a great deal of breath control, partly because of the juxtaposition of short and long lines which need to balance, and partly because of the running on of sense from line to line, the end of each line being masked with a fractional suspension. Do not try to do too much on one breath because it needs to be smooth so that you never want to run out completely. The more familiar you are with it, the more precise you can be with the image, and the more you realise that one image leads into the next. There is a story — a plot if you like — which has to be extracted and made absolutely clear, at the same time as allowing the pictures to spill out and impinge with their seemingly incredible spontaneity. In other words you have to keep the thread of the story clear through all the exotic description. Do not try to make it exotic — it is; the words themselves will make you able to be extravagant. The extravagance contains a certain gentleness. It is excellent material to experiment with range, for it is marvellous musical stuff requiring as much range as you can get, yet keeping it at the same time logically precise.

4 Extract from *Rape of Lucrece*. This is splendid narrative material, difficult to manage because of the number and length of the parentheses. You have to unravel the story and clarify it for the listener, yet allow the descriptive words and phrases to have their full value and be precise; for it is through the measure of the images that we are taken into that heroic world. For example:

> Look as the fair and fiery-pointed sun,
> Rushing from forth a cloud, bereaves our sight;
> Even so . . . .

He takes time off to describe one thing — that is, the sun — so that what is actual, that is, Lucrece behind the curtain can be emphasised:

> Even so the curtain drawn, his eyes begun
> To wink, being blinded with a greater light.

These parentheses are difficult to manage because they must stand as images and yet are part of the story and must further it. They happen all the way through:

> And they [his veins] like straggling slaves for pillage
> fighting
> Obdurate vassals fell exploits effecting . . .
> Swell in their pride, the onset still expecting.

81

That is an extraordinary description. It is through the extravagance of these images that we arrive at an understanding of that passion at its heroic level. There is also present the philosophical comment of the writer observing the situation:

> O had they [Tarquin's eyes] in that darksome prison died,
> Then had they seen the period of their ill.
> Then Collatine again by Lucrece' side,
> In his clear bed might have reposed still.

You will find that the more accurate you are in observing the structure and function of the verse and of the phrasing the more you will convey.

5 Extract from *Absalom and Achitophel*. This is the beginning of a long poem of Dryden's which deals with the intrigues of the Titus Oates plot in the reign of Charles II. Although it is obviously richer if you know something of the historical background, it is understandable up to where I have taken it with the key that is given. It does not present breathing problems as the sense phrases are mainly contained within the couplet; it is the management of the couplet that is difficult. It must never sound repetitive and, therefore, you have to be sensitive to the different movements and rhythms within it. Its value is that it makes you aware of the importance of absolute precision of diction. The humour will not come out by stress. The language is not muscular like that in the other passages because it is too sophisticated. The words themselves are loaded and their particular measure has to be found. The writing is incredibly witty. The opening couplet is loaded with comment on the established church:

> In pious times ere priestcraft did begin,
> Before polygamy was made a sin;

Dryden's attitude to the Church and the morals of the Court is made clear in his particular choice of word:

> When nature prompted, and no law denied
> Promiscuous use of concubine and bride;
> Then Israel's monarch after Heaven's own heart,
> His vigorous warmth did variously impart
> To wives and slaves; and wide as his command,
> Scattered his Maker's image through the land.

Think of what is implicit in the words 'nature prompted', 'vigorous warmth', 'did variously impart', 'A soil ungrateful to the tiller's care': what nicety they have and yet how devastating they are. Yet the whole is so *cool*. Through praise he manages to condemn; through restraint he manages to be vicious; and through being cool he conveys his own smouldering passion. Vocally there is a story to tell, words to investigate, and Dryden's own bitingly ironic observations to be made:

> What faults he [Absalom] had (for who from faults is
> free?)

or:

> But when to sin our biassed nature leans,
> The careful devil is still at hand with means;
> And providently pimps for ill desires:

Vocally this is very demanding.

6 *Over Sir John's Hill.* As I have said, every Dylan Thomas piece is splendid for finding what you can do with the voice, for it increases one's awareness of what sound can do. This passage is particularly difficult for breathing as the breathing and the sense are interwoven. You must observe the form to get the particular feeling of freedom and flight, yet you have to be careful to pursue the sense and to keep the footholds of the plot in front of your audience. 'Over Sir John's Hill, The hawk . . . hangs still.' Here is the description of the hawk and the involved imagery of death and justice — 'black cap', 'fiery tyburn' and so on. There is also the poet and the heron observing, recording and 'graving' the elegy:

> . . . . . .and I who hear the tune of the slow
> Wear-willow river, grave,
> Before the lunge of the night, the notes on this time-shaken
> Stone for the sake of the souls of the slain birds sailing.

There is so much sense and sound, and so many turns in each stanza.

ODE TO THE WEST WIND

i.

O wild West Wind, thou breath of Autumn's being,
Thou from whose unseen presence the leaves dead
Are driven like ghosts from an enchanter fleeing,

Yellow, and black, and pale, and hectic red,
Pestilence-stricken multitudes! O thou
Who chariotest to their dark wintry bed

The wingèd seeds, where they lie cold and low,
Each like a corpse within its grave, until
Thine azure sister of the Spring shall blow

Her clarion o'er the dreaming earth, and fill
(Driving sweet buds like flocks to feed in air)
With living hues and odours plain and hill;

Wild Spirit, which art moving everywhere;
Destroyer and preserver; hear, oh, hear!

ii.

Thou on whose stream, 'mid the steep sky's commotion,
Loose clouds like earth's decaying leaves are shed,
Shook from the tangled boughs of heaven and ocean,

Angels of rain and lightning! there are spread
On the blue surface of thine airy surge,
Like the bright hair uplifted from the head

Of some fierce Maenad, even from the dim verge
Of the horizon to the zenith's height,
The locks of the approaching storm. Thou dirge

Of the dying year, to which this closing night
Will be the dome of a vast sepulchre,
Vaulted with all thy congregated might

Of vapours, from whose solid atmosphere
Black rain, and fire, and hail will burst: oh, hear!

84

Thou who didst waken from his summer dreams
The blue Mediterranean, where he lay,
Lull'd by the coil of his crystalline streams,

Beside a pumice isle in Baiae's bay,
And saw in sleep old palaces and towers
Quivering within the wave's intenser day,

All overgrown with azure moss, and flowers
So sweet, the sense faints picturing them! Thou
For whose path the Atlantic's level powers

Cleave themselves into chasms, while far below
The sea-blooms and the oozy woods which wear
The sapless foliage of the ocean, know

Thy voice, and suddenly grow grey with fear,
And tremble and despoil themselves: oh, hear!

iv.

If I were a dead leaf thou mightest bear;
If I were a swift cloud to fly with thee;
A wave to pant beneath thy power, and share

The impulse of thy strength, only less free
Than thou, O uncontrollable! If even
I were as in my boyhood, and could be

The comrade of thy wanderings over heaven,
As then, when to outstrip thy skiey speed
Scarce seem'd a vision — I would ne'er have striven

As thus with thee in prayer in my sore need.
O! lift me as a wave, a leaf, a cloud!
I fall upon the thorns of life! I bleed!

A heavy weight of hours has chain'd and bow'd
One too like thee — tameless, and swift, and proud.

Make me thy lyre, even as the forest is:
What if my leaves are falling like its own?
The tumult of thy mighty harmonies

Will take from both a deep autumnal tone,
Sweet though in sadness. Be thou, Spirit fierce,
My Spirit! Be thou me, impetuous one!

Drive my dead thoughts over the universe,
Like wither'd leaves, to quicken a new birth;
And, by the incantation of this verse,

Scatter, as from an unextinguish'd hearth
Ashes and sparks, my words among mankind!
Be through my lips to unawaken'd earth

The trumpet of a prophecy! O Wind,
If Winter comes, can Spring be far behind?

Shelley

From *UNDER MILK WOOD*

First Voice

To begin at the beginning:

It is spring, moonless night in the small town, starless and
bible-black, the cobblestreets silent and the hunched, courters'-
and-rabbits' wood limping invisible down to the sloeblack, slow,
black, crowblack, fishingboat-bobbing sea. The houses are blind
as moles (though moles see fine tonight in the snouting, velvet
dingles) or blind as Captain Cat there in the muffled middle by
the pump and the town clock, the shops in mourning, the
Welfare Hall in widows' weeds. And all the people of the lulled
and dumbfound town are sleeping now.

Hush, the babies are sleeping, the farmers, the fishers, the
tradesmen and pensioners, cobbler, schoolteacher, postman and
publican, the undertaker and the fancy woman, drunkard,
dressmaker, preacher, policeman, the webfoot cocklewomen
and the tidy wives. Young girls lie bedded soft or glide in their
dreams, with rings and trousseaux, bridesmaided by glow-worms
down the aisles of the organplaying wood. The boys are dreaming wicked or of the bucking ranches of the night and the
jollyrodgered sea. And the anthracite statues of the horses sleep
in the fields, and the cows in the byres, and the dogs in the
wetnosed yards; and the cats nap in the slant corners or lope
sly, streaking and needling, on the one cloud of the roofs.

You can hear the dew falling, and the hushed town breathing.
Only *your* eyes are unclosed to see the black and folded town
fast, and slow, asleep. And you alone can hear the invisible
starfall, the darkest-before-dawn minutely dewgrazed stir of the
black, dab-filled sea where the *Arethusa*, the *Curlew* and the
Skylark, Zanzibar, Rhiannon, the *Rover,* the *Cormorant,* and
the *Star of Wales* tilt and ride.

Listen. It is night moving in the streets, the processional
salt slow musical wind in Coronation Street and Cockle Row, it
is the grass growing on Llaregyb Hill, dewfall, starfall, the sleep
of birds in Milk Wood.

Listen. It is night in the chill, squat chapel, hymning in
bonnet and brooch and bombazine black, butterfly choker and
bootlace bow, coughing like nannygoats, sucking mintoes, forty-
winking hallelujah; night in the four-ale, quiet as a domino; in
Ocky Milkman's lofts like a mouse with gloves; in Dai Bread's
bakery flying like black flour. It is to-night in Donkey Street,
trotting silent, with seaweed on its hooves, along the cockled
cobbles, past curtained fern-pot, text and trinket, harmonium,

holy dresser, watercolours done by hand, china dog and rosy tin teacaddy. It is night neddying among the snuggeries of babies.

Look. It is night, dumbly, royally winding through the Coronation cherry trees; going through the graveyard of Bethesda with winds gloved and folded, and dew doffed; tumbling by the Sailors Arms.

Time passes. Listen. Time passes.

Come closer now.

Only you can hear the houses sleeping in the streets in the slow deep salt and silent black, bandaged night. Only you can see, in the blinded bedrooms, the combs and petticoats over the chairs, the jugs and basins, the glasses of teeth, Thou Shalt Not on the wall, and the yellowing dickybird-watching pictures of the dead. Only you can hear and see, behind the eyes of the sleepers, the movements and countries and mazes and colours and dismays and rainbows and tunes and wishes and flight and fall and despairs and big seas of their dreams.

From where you are, you can hear their dreams.

Dylan Thomas

From *EPITHALAMION*

My love is now awake out of her dreame,
And her fair eyes, like stars that dimmèd were
With darksome cloud, now show theyr goodly beames
More bright then Hesperus his head doth rere.
Come now, ye damzels, daughters of delight,
Helpe quickly her to dight:
But first come ye fayre hours, which were begot
In Joves sweet Paradice of Day and Night;
Which doe the seasons of the year allot,
And al, that ever in this world is fayre,
Doe make and still repayre:
And ye three handmayds of the Cyprian Queene,
The which doe still adorne her beauties pride,
Helpe to adorne my beautifullest bride:
And, as ye her array, still throwe betweene
Some graces to be seene;
And, as ye use to Venus, to her sing,
The whiles the woods shal answer, and your eccho ring.

Now is my love all ready forth to come:
Let all the virgins therefore well awayt:
And ye fresh boyes, that tend upon her groome,
Prepare your selves; for he is coming strayt.
Set all your things in seemly good aray,
Fit for so joyfull day:
The joyfulst day that ever sunne did see.
Faire Sun! shew forth thy favourable ray,
And let thy lifull heat not fervent be,
For feare of burning her sunshiny face,
Her beauty to disgrace.
O fayrest Phoebus! father of the Muse!
If ever I did honour thee aright,
Or sing the thing that mote thy mind delight,
Doe not thy servants simple boone refuse;
But let this day, let this one day, be myne;
Let all the rest be thine.
Then I thy soverayne praises loud will sing,
That all the woods shal answer, and theyr eccho ring.

Harke! how the Minstrels gin to shrill aloud
Their merry Musick that resounds from far,
The pipe, the tabor, and the trembling Croud,
That well agree withouten breach or jar.
But, most of all, the Damzels doe delite
When they their tymbrels smite,
And thereunto doe daunce and carroll sweet,
That all the sences they doe ravish quite;
The whyles the boyes run up and down the street,
Crying aloud with strong confusèd noyce,
As if it were one voyce,
Hymen, io Hymen, Hymen they do shout;
That even to the heavens theyr shouting shrill
Doth reach, and all the firmament doth fill;
To which the people standing all about,
As in approvance doe thereto applaud,
And loud advance her laud;
And evermore they Hymen, Hymen sing,
That al the woods them answer, and their eccho ring.

Loe! where she comes along with portly pace
Lyke Phoebe, from her chamber of the East,
Arysing forth to run her mighty race,
Clad all in white, that seems a virgin best,
So well it her beseemes, that ye would weene
Some angell she had beene.
Her long loose yellow lockes lyke golden wyre,
Sprinckled with perle, and perling flowres atweene,
Doe lyke a golden mantle her attyre;
And, being crownèd with a girland greene,
Seeme lyke some mayden Queene.
Her modest eyes, abashèd to behold
So many gazers as on her do stayre,
Upon the lowly ground affixèd are;
Ne dare lift up her countenance too bold,
But blush to heare her prayses sung so loud,
So farre from being proud.
Nathless do ye still loud her prayses sing,
That al the woods may answer, and your eccho ring.

Tell me, ye merchants daughters, did ye see
So fayre a creature in your towne before;
So sweet, so lovely, and so mild as she,
Adorned with beautyes grace and vertues store?
Her goodly eyes lyke Saphyres shining bright,
Her forehead yvory white,
Her cheekes lyke apples which the sun hath rudded,
Her lips lyke cherryes charming men to byte,
Her brest lyke to a bowle of creame uncrudded,
Her paps lyke lyllies budded,
Her snowie necke lyke to a marble towre;
And all her body like a pallace fayre,
Ascending up, with many a stately stayre,
To honours seat and chastities sweet bowre.
Why stand ye still ye virgins in amaze,
Upon her so to gaze,
While ye forget your former lay to sing,
To which the woods did answer, and your eccho ring?

But if ye saw that which no eyes can see,
The inward beauty of her lively spright,
Garnisht with heavenly guifts of high degree,
Much more then would ye wonder at that sight,
And stand astonisht lyke to those which red
Medusaes mazeful hed.
There dwels sweet love, and constant chastity,
Unspotted fayth, and comely womanhood,
Regard of honour, and mild modesty;
There vertue raynes as Queen in royal throne,
And giveth lawes alone,
The which the base affections doe obey,
And yeeld theyr services unto her will;
No thought of thing uncomely ever may
Thereto approach to tempt her mind to ill.
Had ye once seen these her celestial threasures,
And unrevealèd pleasures,
Then would ye wonder, and her prayses sing,
That al the woods shal answer, and your eccho ring.

Open the temple gates unto my love,
Open them wide that she may enter in,
And all the postes adorne as doth behove,
And all the pillours deck with girlands trim,
For to receyve this Saynt with honour due,
That commeth in to you.
With trembling steps, and humble reverence,
She commeth in, before th' Almightys view;
Of her ye virgins learn obedience,
When so ye come into those holy places,
To humble your proud faces:
Bring her up to th'high altar, that she may
The sacred ceremonies there partake,
The which doe endlesse matrimonie make;
And let the roaring Organs loudly play
The praises of the Lord in lively notes;
The whiles, with hollow throates,
The Choristers the joyous Antheme sing,
That al the woods may answer and their eccho ring.

Edmund Spenser

From *THE RAPE OF LUCRECE*

Now is he come unto the chamber door
That shuts him from the heaven of his thought,
Which with a yielding latch, and with no more,
Hath barr'd him from the blessed thing he sought.
So from himself impiety hath wrought
    That for his prey to pray he doth begin,
    As if the heavens should countenance his sin.

But in the midst of his unfruitful prayer,
Having solicited th'eternal power,
That his foul thoughts might compass his fair fair,
And they would stand auspicious to the hour,
Even there he starts — quoth he 'I must deflower.
    The powers to whom I pray abhor this fact;
    How can they then assist me in the act?

'Then Love and Fortune be my gods, my guide!
My will is back'd with resolution.
Thoughts are but dreams till their effects be tried;
The blackest sin is clear'd with absolution;
Against love's fire fear's frost hath dissolution.
    The eye of heaven is out, and misty night
    Covers the shame that follows sweet delight'.

This said, his guilty hand pluck'd up the latch,
And with his knee the door he opens wide.
The dove sleeps fast that this night-owl will catch.
Thus treason works ere traitors be espied.
Who sees the lurking serpent steps aside:
    But she, sound sleeping, fearing no such thing,
    Lies at the mercy of his mortal sting.

Into the chamber wickedly he stalks,
And gazeth on her yet unstained bed.
The curtains being close, about he walks,
Rolling his greedy eyeballs in his head.
By their high treason is his heart misled,
    Which gives the watchword to his hand full soon
    To draw the cloud that hides the silver moon.

Look as the fair and fiery-pointed sun,
Rushing from forth a cloud, bereaves our sight;
Even so, the curtain drawn, his eyes begun
To wink, being blinded with a greater light;
Whether it is that she reflects so bright
    That dazzleth them, or else some shame supposed;
    But blind they are, and keep themselves enclosed.

O, had they in that darksome prison died,
Then had they seen the period of their ill!
Then Collatine again by Lucrece' side
In his clear bed might have reposed still;
But they must ope, this blessed league to kill;
    And holy-thoughted Lucrece to their sight,
    Must sell her joy, her life, her world's delight.

Her lily hand her rosy cheek lies under,
Coz'ning the pillow of a lawful kiss;
Who, therefore angry, seems to part in sunder,
Swelling on either side to want his bliss;
Between whose hills her head entombed is;
    Where, like a virtuous monument, she lies,
    To be admir'd by lewd unhallowed eyes.

Without the bed her other fair hand was,
On the green coverlet; whose perfect white
Show'd like an April daisy on the grass,
With pearly sweet, resembling dew of night.
Her eyes, like marigolds, had sheath'd their light,
    And canopied in darkness sweetly lay,
    Till they might open to adorn the day.

Her hair, like golden threads, play'd with her breath —
O modest wantons! wanton modesty! —
Showing life's triumph in the map of death,
And death's dim look in life's mortality.
Each in her sleep themselves so beautify
    As if between them twain there were no strife,
  . But that life liv'd in death, and death in life.

Her breasts, like ivory globes circled with blue,
A pair of maiden worlds unconquered,
Save of their lord no bearing yoke they knew,
And him by oath they truly honoured.
These worlds in Tarquin new ambition bred,
    Who like a foul usurper went about
    From this fair throne to heave the owner out.

What could he see but mightily he noted?
What did he note but strongly he desired?
What he beheld, on that he firmly doted,
And in his will his wilful eye he tired.
With more than admiration he admired
    Her azure veins, her alabaster skin,
    Her coral lips, her snow-white dimpled chin.

As the grim lion fawneth o'er his prey,
Sharp hunger by the conquest satisfied,
So o'er this sleeping soul doth Tarquin stay,
His rage of lust by gazing qualified;
Slack'd, not suppress'd; for standing by her side,
    His eye, which late this mutiny restrains,
    Unto a greater uproar tempts his veins.

And they, like straggling slaves for pillage fighting,
Obdurate vassals fell exploits effecting,
In bloody death and ravishment delighting,
Nor children's tears nor mothers' groans respecting,
Swell in their pride, the onset still expecting,
    Anon his beating heart, alarum striking,
    Gives the hot charge and bids them do their liking.

                         Shakespeare

From *ABSALOM AND ACHITOPHEL*

In pious times ere priestcraft did begin,
Before polygamy was made a sin;
When man on many multiplied his kind.
Ere one to one was cursedly confined;
When nature prompted, and no law denied
Promiscuous use of concubine and bride;
Then Israel's monarch after Heaven's own heart,
His vigorous warmth did variously impart
To wives and slaves; and wide as his command,
Scattered his Maker's image through the land.
Michal, of royal blood, the crown did wear;
A soil ungrateful to the tiller's care:
Not so the rest; for several mothers bore
To god-like David several sons before:
But since like slaves his bed they did ascend,
No true succession could their seed attend.
Of all this numerous progeny was none
So beautiful, so brave, as Absalom:
Whether, inspired by some diviner lust,
His father got him with a greater gust:
Or that his conscious destiny made way,
By manly beauty, to imperial sway.
Early in foreign fields he won renown
With kings and states allied to Israel's crown:
In peace the thoughts of war he could remove,
And seemed as he were only born for love.
Whate'er he did, was done with so much ease,
In him alone 'twas natural to please:
His motions all accompanied with grace;
And paradise was opened in his face.
With secret joy indulgent David viewed
His youthful image in his son renewed:
To all his wishes nothing he denied;
And made the charming Annabel his bride.
What faults he had (for who from faults is free?)
His father could not, or he would not see.
Some warm excesses which the law forbore,
Were construed youth that purged by boiling o'er,
And Amnon's murder, by a specious name,
Was called a just revenge for injured fame.
Thus praised and loved, the noble youth remained,
While David, undisturbed, in Sion reigned.
But life can never be sincerely blest:

Heaven punishes the bad, and proves the best.
The Jews, a headstrong, moody, murmuring race,
As ever tried the extent and stretch of grace;
God's pampered people, whom, debauched with ease,
No king could govern, nor no gods could please;
Gods they had tried of every shape and size,
That god-smiths could produce, or priests devise;
These Adam-wits, too fortunately free,
Began to dream they wanted liberty;
And when no rule, no precedent, was found,
Of men, by laws less circumscribed and bound;
They led their wild desires to woods and caves,
And thought that all but savages were slaves.
They who, when Saul was dead, without a blow,
Made foolish Ishbosheth the crown forego;
Who banished David did from Hebron bring,
And with a general shout proclaimed him king:
Those very Jews, who, at their very best,
Their humour more than loyalty expressed,
Now wondered why so long they had obeyed
An idol monarch, which their hands had made;
Thought they might ruin him they could create,
Or melt him to that golden calf — a state.
But these were random bolts: no formed design,
Nor interest made the factious crowd to join:
The sober part of Israel, free from stain,
Well knew the value of a peaceful reign;
And, looking backward with a wise affright,
Saw seams of wounds dishonest to the sight:
In contemplation of whose ugly scars,
They cursed the memory of civil wars.
The moderate sort of men thus qualified,
Inclined the balance to the better side;
And David's mildness managed it so well,
The bad found no occasion to rebel.
But when to sin our biassed nature leans,
The careful devil is still at hand with means;
And providently pimps for ill desires;
The good old cause revived a plot requires.
Plots, true or false, are necessary things,
To raise up commonwealths, and ruin kings.

John Dryden

Characters Represented

David . . . . Charles II
Michal . . . . Queen Catharine
Absalom . . . Duke of Monmouth, natural son to Charles II
Achitophel . . Earl of Shaftesbury
Annabel . . . Anne, Duchess of Monmouth
Saul . . . . . Oliver Cromwell
Ishbosheth . . Richard Cromwell
Israel . . . . England
The Jews . . . The English
Hebron . . . Scotland

Over Sir John's hill,
The hawk on fire hangs still;
In a hoisted cloud, at drop of dusk, he pulls to his claws
And gallows, up the rays of his eyes the small birds of the bay
And the shrill child's play
Wars
Of the sparrows and such who swansing, dusk, in wrangling
                                        hedges.

And blithely they squawk
To fiery tyburn over the wrestle of elms until
The flash the noosed hawk
Crashes, and slowly the fishing holy stalking heron
In the river Towy below bows his tilted headstone.

Flash, and the plumes crack,
And a black cap of jack-
Daws Sir John's just hill dons, and again the gulled birds hare
To the hawk on fire, the halter height, over Towy's fins,
In a whack of wind.
There
Where the elegiac fisherbird stabs and paddles
In the pebbly dab-filled
Shallow and sedge, and 'dilly dilly,' calls the loft hawk,
'Come and be killed,'
I open the leaves of the water at a passage
Of psalms and shadows among the pincered sandcrabs prancing

And read, in a shell,
Death clear as a buoy's bell:
All praise of the hawk on fire in hawk-eyed dusk be sung,
When his viperish fuse hangs looped with flames under the brand
Wing, and blest shall
Young
Green chickens of the bay and bushes cluck, 'dilly dilly,
Come let us die.'
We grieve as the blithe birds, never again, leave shingle and elm,
The heron and I,
I young Aesop fabling to the near night by the dingle
Of eels, saint heron hymning in the shell-hung distant

Crystal harbour vale
Where the sea cobbles sail,
And wharves of water where the walls dance and the white
                                          cranes stilt.
It is the heron and I, under judging Sir John's elmed
Hill, tell-tale the knelled
Guilt
Of the led-astray birds whom God, for their breast of whistles,
Have mercy on,
God in his whirlwind silence save, who marks the sparrows hail,
For their souls' song.
Now the heron grieves in the weeded verge. Through windows
Of dusk and water I see the tilting whispering

Heron, mirrored, go.
As the snapt feathers snow,
Fishing in the tear of the Towy. Only a hoot owl
Hollows, a grassblade blown in cupped hands, in the looted elms
And no green cocks or hens
Shout
Now on Sir John's hill. The heron, ankling the scaly
Lowlands of the waves,
Makes all the music; and I who hear the tune of the slow,
Wear-willow river, grave,
Before the lunge of the night, the notes on this time-shaken
Stone for the sake of the souls of the slain birds sailing.

Dylan Thomas

Use this material to join up the whole mechanism and to discover
the range and power you have. When you are working try to lose all
preconceptions of how it should sound for this is a false security.
Start from scratch and begin to hear the possibilities in your voice
and in the text you are using. It should be a physical and mental
loosening of yourself so that you are ready for the moment and you
can surprise yourself, for each moment is different. It is like walking
a tightrope: some bits go well and some bits will be disappointing,
but that does not matter. The important thing is that what is heard
is true of you. The aim is effortlessness so that you are free to let
your thought and feelings out. If there is effort in the voice you
cannot be free to do this.

5 Speaking Poetry

As so much of the material I have given is poetry, I would like to say one or two quite straightforward things about speaking poetry.

The main purpose of speaking poetry so far has been to get the voice free. Simply by speaking it with a certain enquiry you learn a lot about it. But its value to the actor, whether or not you are going to do Shakespeare or other poetic drama, is that it increases this sensibility to words, and rhythms and meanings which come to you from sound — meanings which cannot necessarily be explained and which go deeper than our conscious logical mind. These meanings come from a precise choice of words and their associations. (Thomas Mann said that 'associations' was the most important word in the vocabulary.) The particularness of the word is one of the crucial things for an actor to realise as it will affect his work whether he is using prose or poetry.

I think actors are very often frightened of tackling poetry, feeling that there is some sort of mystique about it, some *way* of doing it. If this is the case, one of two things may happen: either you are over-reverent about it, and the 'poetry voice' happens; or, in rebelling against the 'poetry voice' you ignore the form and go only for the logical sense, and the poetry then sounds like prose. Of course, neither need happen. It is a question of finding the balance between the formal and the informal, the colloquial and the heightened language. The American poet Lawrence Ferlinghetti said that the poet is the 'super-realist', and if you think about it, that is the key.

I would like to say something quite simple to start with about metre and rhythm, for I think a confusion about dealing with this often causes concern. The following extract from the very metrical verse of Longfellow's *Hiawatha* is a very crude example of what I mean:

> First he dánced a sólemn méasure,
> Véry slów in stép and gésture,
> Ín and oút among the píne-trees,
> Tréading sóftly líke a pánther.
> Thén more swíftly ánd still swífter,
> Whírling, spínning roúnd in círcles,
> Tíll the léaves went whírling wíth him,
> Tíll the dúst and léaves togéther
> Spréad in éddies roúnd abóut him.

There is nothing remarkable here about the content or the imagery

101

but you will see that I have marked the metrical stress. There are
four beats to each line and each beat has one stressed and one
unstressed syllable. If you read it aloud the metrical pattern is
obvious. The metrical stress does not always coincide with the sense
stress, so to stress it only metrically makes nonsense of the sense.
How do you manage this? If you take it that each line has four ounces
of stress, and that that weight in stress can be disposed as you wish
through the line, then interesting things can happen to the sense,
and you might get stressing something like this:

> First he danced a solemn measure,
> Very slow in step and gesture,
> In and out among the pine-trees,
> Treading softly like a panther.
> Then more swiftly and still swifter,
> Whirling, spinning round in circles,
> Till the leaves went whirling with him,
> Till the dust and leaves together
> Spread in eddies round about him.

This is one way of stressing it, but by no means the only way. As long
as you take the same time for each line as when you are stressing it
metrically, and the same weight of stress on each line, you can put
that stress where you wish. There are countless permutations of
rhythm where the sense stress and the metre stress go against each
other, and enable you to stretch or shorten words as you wish — that
is, to syncopate them. It is, therefore, possible to make the movement
different in each line, while preserving the weight of stress, and to
alight on words in order to emphasize them. You will notice that
some lines have only two or three stresses and some have their full
quota of stressed words. If you make less than the metrical stresses
it means that you can linger on and stretch a word. It is then that
your choice becomes important, for it is that choice that will
enlighten your audience as to the meaning. If you said the lines only
for the sense, taking no account of the metrical structure, the result
would bear little relation to the poem.

   This is, as I have said, a crude example, but it clarifies what can
happen. When you are dealing with poetry written in a much more
sophisticated and subtle way, with imagery, associations of words,
internal rhythms and all the devices a poet uses, then the whole thing
becomes wide open with possibilities. It is then that you have to
start to listen, for it is through listening for what the text contains
that you will hear its possibilities.

   If you look back at the little Herrick lyric *Bid me to live*, which
you have already thought of in terms of its vowels and consonants,

you will see that it is also metrically exact. It has alternately four and three beats to a line, eight and six consonants, and is absolutely regular. But when you read it through you will find how the movement of the lines quite miraculously changes within its strict time.

> Bid me to live, and I will live
> Thy Protestant to be;
> Or bid me love, and I will give
> A loving heart to thee.

The first line breaks in the middle and the end of the line lifts and runs on into the next to allow the rhythm of that whole line to gather on the word 'Protestant' which takes all the stress of that line. 'Protestant' was a loaded word to use in those days, and an extraordinary one to include in a secular love poem. Suspending the end of the line in this way in order to mark it underlines the stress in the next line. The following two lines are very much the same in movement except that the word 'Or' at the beginning changes the texture very slightly by relating this to the first line but at the same time carrying on to a new thought. Also, the rhythm of the last line is not as unusual as that of the second line because there is not so much to notice.

> A heart as soft, a heart as kind,
> A heart as sound and free
> As in the whole world thou canst find,
> That heart I'll give to thee.

This is quite a different movement. There is a build-up through the first three lines, with the emphasis on the nature of the heart. All the stress is on those descriptive words, which also happen to have open, long vowels — 'soft', 'kind', 'sound', 'free'. Each descriptive word leads on to the next, the rhythm taking you forward and making you wait until the third line before you are allowed to come to rest. The rhythm of the whole line is gathered on the words 'whole world' and, because the sense of the previous two lines has been run on, the weight is that much greater when you alight on those two words. The last line is, of necessity, evenly stressed to bring the whole verse together. The next three verses are fairly regular:

> Bid that heart stay, and it will stay
> To honour thy decree:
> Or bid it languish quite away,
> And't shall do so for thee.

Bid me to weep, and I will weep,
　　While I have eyes to see:
And, having none, yet will I keep
　　A heart to weep for thee.

Bid me despair, and I'll despair,
　　Under that Cypress-tree:
Or bid me die, and I will dare
　　E'en death, to die for thee.

These verses are quite regular in rhythm, though the texture differs
with each thing said; each request leads to another, more excessive
than the last, until you reach 'Or bid me die', the ultimate
extravagance. After this comes the very major formal statement of
the end, which resolves the meaning and the sound of the poem:

Thou art my life, my love, my heart,
　　The very eyes of me:
And hast command of every part,
　　To live and die for thee.

Everyone will vary in what balance of stress they wish to give the
poem, and what cadence they hear, and this is as it should be. The
important thing is that you listen precisely to the measure and tension
of the words because they are always the key.

It is splendid to read Herrick aloud, for he makes you very sensitive
to the sophisticated pleasure in rhythm. The discipline is in the
structure and the freedom is in the enormous variety of weight,
length and cadence he allows the words. *Corinna's Going A Maying*
is much more complex in structure and much deeper in content.
When you read it aloud, the effect of running on the sense from line
to line is obvious – it gives the poem an incredible sense of gaiety.
If you do not mark the end of the line by a slight suspension you
lose the gaiety because the balance of the lines is lost. You also
lose the pleasure in the rhythm which should not be underestimated.
The whole piece is overflowing with images, all of which have to be
precise. The heightened imagery contains part of the humour. In the
line ' 'tis sin – Nay, profanation to keep in', the extravagant word
'profanation' is its precise religious meaning being used in a secular
context. Notice how you are held up after ' 'tis sin' as the line lifts
and suspends a fraction before it goes into the next line. Here you
are made to wait again by 'Nay', and a comma; you are then
brought right down on to: ' 'Tis profanation to keep in'. The whole
poem is full of such ingenuity. In addition, there is throughout an
amazing balance of the colloquial language of the time and formal

structure. This balance is always shifting so that you have to be continually alive to it. The message on the surface is 'Hurry up; do not waste time, let us enjoy ourselves while we can' and so on. Just below the surface, however, the rhythm is telling you something quite different, something of the inevitability of death.

In the last verse the incantational sound, with its implicit reference to the beginnings of poetry in chanting spells, takes over and it makes you aware of man's mortal position in the eternal universe. It has an atavistic sound which connects us with our beginnings and with the inevitability of our end — 'and we are but decaying'. The whole sound of this last verse changes and, without having to explain anything, it takes you into another area of understanding, a deeper reality.

This brings you to one of the most valuable discoveries in poetry: an awareness of how sound can take you into another territory, not logically, for it does not need to explain anything. Purely by the associations of words and rhythms it can penetrate the subconscious understanding. Language itself reacts on us.

CORINNA'S GOING A MAYING

Get up, get up for shame, the Blooming Morn
Upon her wings presents the god unshorn.
    See how Aurora throws her fair
    Fresh-quilted colours through the air:
    Get up, sweet Slug-a-bed, and see
    The Dew-bespangling Herb and Tree.
Each Flower has wept, and bowed toward the East,
Above an hour since; yet you not drest,
    Nay! not so much as out of bed?
    When all the Birds have Mattens said,
    And sung their thankful Hymns: 'tis sin
    Nay, profanation to keep in,
When as a thousand Virgins on this day,
Spring, sooner than the Lark, to fetch in May.

Rise; and put on your Foliage, and be seen
To come forth, like the Spring-time, fresh and green;
 And sweet as Flora. Take no care
 For Jewels for your Gown, or Hair:
 Fear not; the leaves will strew
 Gems in abundance upon you:
Besides, the childhood of the Day has kept,
Against you come, some Orient Pearls unwept:
 Come, and receive them while the light
 Hangs on the Dew-locks of the night:
 And Titan on the Eastern hill
 Retires himself, or else stands still
Till you come forth. Wash, dress, be brief in praying:
Few Beads are best, when once we go a Maying.

Come, my Corinna, come; and coming, mark
How each field turns a street; each street a Park
 Made green, and trimmed with trees: see how
 Devotion gives each House a Bough,
 Or Branch: each porch, each door, ere this
 An Ark a Tabernacle is
Made up of white-thorn neatly interwove;
As if here were those cooler shades of love.
 Can such delights be in the street,
 And open fields, and we not see't?
 Come, we'll abroad; and let's obey
 The Proclamation made for May:
And sin no more, as we have done, by staying;
But my Corinna, come, let's go a Maying.

There's not a budding Boy, or Girl, this day,
But is got up, and gone to bring in May.
 A deal of Youth, ere this, is come
 Back, and with White-thorn laden home.
 Some have dispatcht their Cakes and Cream,
 Before that we have left to dream:
And some have wept, and wooed, and plighted Troth,
And chose their Priest, ere we can cast off sloth:
 Many a green-gown has been given;
 Many a kiss, both odd and even:
 Many a glance too has been sent
 From out the eye, Love's Firmament:
Many a jest told of the Keyes betraying
This night, and Locks pickt, yet we're not a Maying.

Come, let us go, while we are in our prime;
And take the harmless folly of the time.
We shall grow old apace, and die
Before we know our liberty.
Our life is short; and our days run
As fast away as does the Sun:
And as a vapour, or a drop of rain
Once lost, can ne'er be found again:
So when or you or I are made
A fable, song, or fleeting shade;
All love, all liking, all delight
Lies drowned with us in endless night.
Then while time serves, and we are but decaying;
Come, my Corinna, come, let's go a Maying.

Robert Herrick

The following Hopkins poem is something totally different, both
in its rhythm and the tension of its words. It is written in what is
called Sprung Rhythm which, very crudely, is this: there are a
given number of stresses in the line (in this case it is a sonnet so
there are five) but the number of unstressed syllables can vary.
This means that some lines can be very full and others quite
spare and the effects can be astonishing. For instance, in Hopkins's
sonnet *Spring* you have a line with three strong stresses one after
the other:

. . . . . . it strikes like lightnings to hear him sing;

The three stresses on 'strikes like lightnings', in context with the
liquid rich sound of the beginning of the sonnet, make the line
quite remarkable. Of course, the Sprung Rhythm, with its counter-
point, is very complicated. It evolved out of early Saxon poetry
and uses a good deal of alliteration and assonance. In order to be
thorough about it you need to read Hopkins's notes and go through
the poems carefully; much has been written on the subject and
the more you know about it the more you realize that its com-
plexity is bound up with what he is trying to communicate. My
purpose in choosing it is to look at what he makes some of the
words do. The valuable thing an actor learns from Hopkins is that
the energy the words have of themselves contains the particular
stress that is in his meaning. That energy is directly related to the
way the words are made. So that, in fact, you cannot really use
those words if you are not aware of the separate energy it takes

107

to form them.

I have marked this sonnet as I think the stress was intended. In some of the poems which are particularly difficult Hopkins puts his own stress marks to guide you. You will see in these next two lines how the choice of rhythm makes him able to vary the quantity and weight of sound in the line:

Mary, mother of us, where is your relief?

My cries heave, herds-long; huddle in a main, a chief —

You are having to listen for a quite different kind of rhythm. In the Herrick piece there was a continual balancing of the metrical and sense stresses, whereas Hopkins lays the stress on the sense for you, to more brutal and less sophisticated effect. This gives the poem an extraordinary force to start with and, most important, it means that if you find that exact energy in its rhythm and in its words you will not have to underline the meaning by being forceful yourself. If you start to emphasize you are lost because you will lose what it is saying. That is, if you try to explain you will confuse, but if you allow the words to do their own work the meaning will be clear. The moral is obvious: if you become emphatic in a text which requires strength you impose something on the text which does not allow your audience to hear the strength within it.

The remarkable thing about Hopkins is that he does not merely describe what something is like but also makes you experience it physically. He does this by various means: word associations, sound associations, using metaphors which mix the senses. He describes one thing in terms of another, the effect of one sense in terms of the reaction of another sense, in order to get at the 'thisness' or essence of what he is describing, so that it is absolutely particular. For instance, in the sonnet *Spring*, he describes thrushes' eggs as looking like 'little low heavens', with all the texture that that image contains, and goes on to describe the sound the thrush makes:

. . . . and thrush
Through the echoing timber does so rinse and wring
The ear, it strikes like lightnings to hear him sing;

He is describing a sound in terms of the strong physical action of rinsing and wringing (both with their associations of cleansing) and in terms of blinding light. The word 'wring', which also has the sound association of ringing bells, makes you understand something

of the pitch of the note, and the two words 'rinse' and 'wring'
together make you aware of its action on the ear. By mixing the
senses in the metaphors in this extraordinary way, you are able to
understand not only what the sound is like but also the experience
of that sound on the ear. In the poem that I have included here
you begin to fathom something of Hopkins's particular despair,
and you understand something of how it affected him physically.
It alerts you to something that I was talking about in the first
chapter — the physical root of words. Take the first line of this
poem:

No worst, there is none. Pitched past pitch of grief.

After the first statement you are plunged straight into his
predicament with the word 'pitched'. There is no pronoun or
anything to guide you in. You are there in his subjective world.
The repetition of the word gives you the feeling that the despair
is endless. The word itself contains three meanings: being thrown
blackness and the texture of pitch itself; and the pitch of a note.
All these physical associations are gathered on one word. In the
line 'on an age-old anvil wince and sing —', the physical distress
of the sound relates to the poet's own despair, and the tension
and weight of the words gives you the measure of that despair.
Again:

O the mind, mind has mountains; cliffs of fall
Frightful, sheer, no-man-fathomed.

This image, in terms of space, danger and mystery is a remarkable
one to use when describing your own mind and the fear of
madness.

Of course, an enormous amount has been, and still can be, said
about Hopkins's poems. What they do for you is open your ears
to another, more brutal way of using words, which takes you into
his private world. Therefore, to be able to use and come to terms
with language like this increases your sensibility as an actor a
hundred per cent. All his poems are, in this way, a kind of
revelation. If you approach the text of this sonnet in a didactic
way saying 'This is what I feel about it, I must make it clear, I must
stress those words, this should be said like this', and so on, you will
be unsuccessful. You must know the text as well as possible, free
yourself of pressure and listen for what that text contains. Allow
yourself to receive the image, the sound and the rhythm before you
give it to the audience, so that however well you know the text
it will always be a discovery. The text will then come out clearly

109

with no pressure and the voice will become alive and make it remarkable.

I also include a passage from Hopkins's notebooks which describes what it is like to be oneself. It helps you to understand his sense of the essence of being and, therefore, the organic necessity for the words he uses.

SONNET

No wórst, there is nóne. Pitched past pítch of gríef,
Móre pangs will, schóoled at fóre-pangs, wílder wríng.
Cómforter, whére, whére is your cómforting?
Máry, mothér of us, whére is yóur relíef?
My criés heáve, hérds-long; húddle in a main, a chief –
Wóe, wórld-sorrow; on an áge-old anvil wínce and síng –
Then lúll, then leáve off. Fúry had shrieked 'No líng-
ering! Lét me be féll: fórce I múst be bríef'.
O the mínd, mínd has móuntains; clíffs of fall
Fríghtful, shéer, ńo-man-fáthomed. Hold them chéap
Máy who ne'er húng there. Nór does lóng our sḿall
Dúrance déal with that stéep or déep. Here! créep,
Wrétch, under a cómfort seŕves in a whírlwind: áll
Lífe déath does énd and each day diés with sleép.

Gerard Manley Hopkins

From *NOTEBOOKS AND PAPERS*

We may learn that all things are created by consideration of the world without or of ourselves the world within. The former is the consideration commonly dwelt upon, but the latter takes on the mind more hold. I find myself both as a man and as myself something most determined and distinctive, at pitch, more distinctive and higher pitched than anything else I see; I find myself with my pleasures and pains, my powers and my experiences, my deserts and guilt, my shame and sense of beauty, my dangers, hopes, fears, and all my fate, more important to myself than anything I see. And when I ask where does all this throng and stack of being, so rich, so distinctive, so important, come from / nothing I see can answer me. And this whether I speak of human nature or of my individuality, my selfbeing. For human nature, being more highly pitched, selved

and distinctive than anything in the world, can have been
developed, evolved, condensed, from the vastness of the
world not anyhow or by the working of common powers but
only by one of finer or higher pitch and determination than
itself and certainly than any that elsewhere we see, for this
power had to force forward the starting or stubborn elements
to the one pitch required. And this is much more true when
we consider the mind; when I consider my selfbeing, my
consciousness and feeling of myself, that taste of myself, of
I and *me* above and in all things, which is more distinctive
than the taste of ale or alum, more distinctive than the smell
of walnutleaf or camphor, and is incommunicable by any
means to another man (as when I was a child I used to ask
myself: What must it be to be someone else?). Nothing else in
nature comes near this unspeakable stress of pitch, distinctive-
ness, and selving, this selfbeing of my own.

Gerard Manley Hopkins

The next poem, *A Nocturnall upon St. Lucies Day*, by Donne, is
also about despair — the despair at the death of someone he loves. He
conveys this despair by considering what it is like to be nothing. It is
only by knowing what *nothing* is that we know the nature of *substance*.
Donne does this by a marvellous extravagance of piling nothing on
nothing: he is the Epitaph of everything that is dead; a quintessence
of Nothingness; the grave of all that's Nothing; the Elixir of Nothing;
and finally 'But I am None. . . '. It is clearly a difficult poem to
unravel. The language astonishes by its colloquialism and originality:
the images are of the universe, alchemy and of the body. Implicit in
metaphysical writing is man's position in the universe, putting man's
feelings in perspective. As you unravel the meaning you hear the
particular intensity of feeling that is contained in the argument. It is
only by being particular about the physical presence of the images
that you understand the measure of this feeling. The value is in
unravelling the meaning and experiencing the sound. You can hear
how the balance of the argument and the 'sing' of the language are
always on a see-saw. You have to continually pursue the argument
while listening for the moments when it needs to sing. Edith Sitwell
said that poetry was a suppressed scream — you need, therefore, to
keep it ordinary until it can no longer be ordinary!

This poem should be said aloud. Do not presuppose anything, but
listen for what it does. It teaches you how to manipulate the colloquial
with the formal and the extravagant with intensity of feeling.

A NOCTURNALL UPON ST. LUCIES DAY

Being the shortest day

Tis the years midnight, and it is the days,
Lucies, who scarce seven hours herself unmasks,
The Sun is spent, and now his flasks
Send forth light squibs, no constant rays;
 The worlds whole sap is sunk:
The generall balm th'hydroptique earth hath drunk,
Whither, as to the beds-feet, life is shrunk,
Dead and enterred; yet all these seem to laugh,
Compared with me, who am their Epitaph.

Study me then, you who shall lovers be
At the next world, that is, at the next Spring:
 For I am every dead thing,
 In whom love wrought new Alchemy.
  For his art did express
A quintessence even from nothingness,
From dull privations, and lean emptiness:
He ruined me, and I am re-begot
Of absence, darkness, death; things which are not.

All others, from all things, draw all that's good,
Life, soul, form, spirit, whence they being have;
 I, by love's limbeck, am the grave
 Of all, that's nothing. Oft a flood
  Have we two wept, and so
Drowned the whole world, us two; oft did we grow
To be two Chaoses, when we did show
Care to aught else; and often absences
Withdrew our souls, and made us carcasses.

But I am by her death, (which word wrongs her)
Of the first nothing, the Elixir grown;
 Were I a man, that I were one,
 I needs must know; I should prefer,
  If I were any beast,
Some ends, some means; Yea plants, yea stones detest,
And love; All, all some properties invest;
If I an ordinary nothing were,
As shadow, a light, and body must be here.

But I am None; nor will my Sun renew:
You lovers, for whose sake, the lesser Sun
   At this time to the Goat is run
   To fetch new lust, and give it you,
      Enjoy your summer all;
Since she enjoys her long nights festival,
Let me prepare towards her, and let me call
This hour her Vigil, and her Eve, since this
Both the years, and the days deep midnight is.

John Donne

A third poem about despair is *The Going* by Hardy, written on the death of his first wife. There is nothing extraordinary about the language; you could read it through quickly and find nothing special in it. But if you read it carefully, observing the form — the delicacy of the rhythm, the suspension of the run-on lines, the balancing of the short lines with the long, the sense pauses in the middle of the lines — you begin to hear a sound which is peculiar to Hardy. The formality of the rhythm and the informality of the language give it a particular tension and dictate a cadence which reveals something of his mind and feelings. Quite ordinary phrases then become remarkable. For example:

You would close your term here, up and be gone

Where I could not follow
With wing of swallow
To gain one glimpse of you ever anon!

or:

. . . while I
Saw morning harden upon the wall,
Unmoved, unknowing
That your great going
Had place that moment, and altered all.

Until the last verse the poem is desolating. The word 'undo' somehow contains all the irony and fatalism that you are aware of in his writing. You have to observe the form and listen for what the words do. If you think of it as being a sad poem the audience will not be able to get at Hardy. Conversely, if you make it too colloquial the full measure of his feeling will be lost.

113

THE GOING

Why did you give no hint that night
That quickly after the morrow's dawn,
And calmly, as if indifferent quite,
You would close your term here, up and be gone
    Where I could not follow
    With wing of swallow
To gain one glimpse of you ever anon!

    Never to bid good-bye,
    Or lip me the softest call,
Or utter a wish for a word, while I
Saw morning harden upon the wall,
    Unmoved, unknowing
    That your great going
Had place that moment, and altered all.

Why do you make me leave the house
And think for a breath it is you I see
At the end of the alley of bending boughs
Where so often at dusk you used to be;
    Till in darkening dankness
    The yawning blankness
Of the perspective sickens me!

    You were she who abode
    By those red-veined rocks far West,
You were the swan-necked one who rode
Along the beetling Beeny Crest,
    And, reining nigh me,
    Would muse and eye me,
While Life unrolled us its very best.

Why, then, latterly did we not speak,
Did we not think of those days long dead,
And ere your vanishing strive to seek
That time 's renewal? We might have said,
    "In this bright spring weather
    We'll visit together
Those places that once we visited."

> Well, well! All's past amend,
> Unchangeable. It must go.
> I seem but a dead man held on end
> To sink down soon . . . . .O you could not know
> That such swift fleeing
> No soul foreseeing ——
> Not even I —— would undo me so!

Thomas Hardy

In the following poem of Yeats there is again a mixture of the colloquial and the formal. Yeats, in this poem about the Easter uprising, plunges you into a world without any explanation, jumping from subject to subject and person to person, making you wait until the end for him to pull the threads together and make sense of the whole. That is why it is so interesting to speak — you have to stun the audience into accepting each new subject or thought which he introduces, so that there are no worries about the progression of the meaning until it is clarified at the end. It needs nerve. The beginning is marvellously eloquent:

> I have met them at close of day
> Coming with vivid faces
> From counter or desk among grey
> Eighteenth-century houses.
> I have passed with a nod of the head
> Or polite meaningless words,
> Or have lingered awhile and said
> Polite meaningless words,
> And thought before I had done
> Of a mocking tale or a gibe
> To please a companion
> Around the fire at the club.

It all but ignores the strong inevitability of the rhythm underneath. But, of course, it does not ignore it completely, because it is the tension created by the rhetoric of the words resisting the incantation of the rhythm that gives it its particular wit and irony. The rhythm starts to take over on:

> Being certain that they and I
> But lived where motley is worn:

and the 'sing' is uppermost on:

> All changed, changed utterly:
> A terrible beauty is born.

The word 'motley' in this context startles you because it not only means a division of colour and therefore of loyalty as opposed to the colour green which symbolised the Irish cause, but it also has its associations with the clown, therefore implying that the world is no more than a circus.

Who is Yeats referring to when he speaks about 'them'? You are taken into a relationship with people without introduction. In the second verse he describes them but does not name them. The language remains rhetorical. You gather it is an elegy — the 'casual comedy' continues the association started by 'motley'. In the third verse he deals with the subconscious effect of a cause on people, how they become bound up with it to the exclusion of all else, which inevitably leads to imbalance. He has stopped mocking and takes you deeper. In consequence, the sound changes. In the last verse he identifies the people and the cause and is quite specific in his questions:

> Was it needless death after all?
> For England may keep faith
> For all that is done and said.

In the last verse the incantation of the rhythm takes over. This has an unusual gentleness. The repetition of the last two lines in the first, second and last verses are quite surprising and have an extraordinary emotional size.

EASTER 1916

> I have met them at close of day
> Coming with vivid faces
> From counter or desk among grey
> Eighteenth-century houses.
> I have passed with a nod of the head
> Or polite meaningless words,
> Or have lingered awhile and said
> Polite meaningless words,
> And thought before I had done
> Of a mocking tale or a gibe
> To please a companion
> Around the fire at the club,
> Being certain that they and I

But lived where motley is worn:
All changed, changed utterly:
A terrible beauty is born.

That woman's days were spent
In ignorant good-will,
Her nights in argument
Until her voice grew shrill.
What voice more sweet than hers
When, young and beautiful,
She rode to harriers?
This man had kept a school
And rode our wingèd horse;
This other his helper and friend
Was coming into his force;
He might have won fame in the end,
So sensitive his nature seemed,
So daring and sweet his thought.
This other man I had dreamed
A drunken, vainglorious lout.
He had done most bitter wrong
To some who are near my heart,
Yet I number him in the song;
He, too, has resigned his part
In the casual comedy;
He, too, has been changed in his turn,
Transformed utterly:
A terrible beauty is born.

Hearts with one purpose alone
Through summer and winter seem
Enchanted to a stone
To trouble the living stream.
The horse that comes from the road,
The rider, the birds that range
From cloud to tumbling cloud,
Minute by minute they change;
A shadow of cloud on the stream
Changes minute by minute;
A horse-hoof slides on the brim,
And a horse plashes within it;
The long-legged moor-hens dive,
And hens to moor-cocks call;
Minute by minute they live:
The stone's in the midst of all.

Too long a sacrifice
Can make a stone of the heart.
O when may it suffice?
That is Heaven's part, our part
To murmur name upon name,
As a mother names her child
When sleep at last has come
On limbs that had run wild.
What is it but nightfall?
No, no, not night but death;
Was it needless death after all?
For England may keep faith
For all that is done and said.
We know their dream; enough
To know they dreamed and are dead;
And what if excess of love
Bewildered them till they died?
I write it out in a verse —
MacDonagh and MacBride
And Connolly and Pearse
Now and in time to be,
Wherever green is worn,
Are changed, changed utterly:
A terrible beauty is born.

W.B. Yeats

The last poem I include here is Lawrence's *Tortoise Shout*. His poetry is seldom pressed into a form. He gets at the same kind of essence as Hopkins, but by accumulation rather than compression. He describes something, adds to that description, qualifies it and adds something else. Then he shifts to another tack altogether until you cumulatively discover something of the essence of what he is describing. In order to find what is there you have to listen and be totally open to receive each impression as it occurs, for there is no formal guide of structure. But the rhythm is there in the short lines, the statements, the questions, the long cumulative run-on lines, shifting from one tack to another, and this gives the poem its particular probing movement. There is also the extraordinary sense of discovery of the separate existence of each thing. With it you can preconceive nothing. You must listen for what it says. Because, in the end, it relates to one's own existence, it can only be given meaning if it is allowed to 'touch down' on one's own private sense of physical being. It is this that must inform the voice.

TORTOISE SHOUT

I thought he was dumb,
I said he was dumb,
Yet I've heard him cry.

First faint scream,
Out of life's unfathomable dawn,
Far off, so far, like a madness, under the horizon's dawning rim,
Far, far off, far scream.

Tortoise *in extremis.*

Why were we crucified into sex?
Why were we not left rounded off, and finished in ourselves,
As we began,
As he certainly began, so perfectly alone?

A far, was-it-audible scream,
Or did it sound on the plasm direct?

Worse than the cry of the new-born,
A scream,
A yell,
A shout,
A paean,
A death-agony,
A birth-cry,
A submission,
All, tiny, far away, reptile under the first dawn.

War-cry, triumph, acute-delight, death-scream reptilian,
Why was the veil torn?
The silken shriek of the soul's torn membrane?
The male soul's membrane
Torn with a shriek half music, half horror.

Crucifixion.
Male tortoise, cleaving behind the hovel-wall of that dense female,
Mounted and tense, spread-eagle, out-reaching out of the shell
In tortoise-nakedness,
Long neck, and long vulnerable limbs extruded, spread-eagle over her
                              house-roof,
And the deep, secret, all-penetrating tail curved beneath her walls,
Reaching and gripping tense, more reaching anguish in uttermost
                              tension

Till suddenly, in the spasm of coition, tupping like a jerking leap,
                                        and oh!
Opening its clenched face from his outstretched neck
And giving that fragile yell, that scream,
Super-audible,
From his pink, cleft, old man's mouth,
Giving up the ghost,
Or screaming in Pentecost, receiving the ghost.

His scream, and his moment's subsidence,
The moment of eternal silence,
Yet unreleased, and after the moment, the sudden, startling jerk of
                                        coition, and at once
The inexpressible faint yell —
And so on, till the last plasm of my body was melted back
To the primeval rudiments of life, and the secret.

So he tups, and screams
Time after time that frail, torn scream
After each jerk, the longish interval,
The tortoise eternity,
Age-long reptilian persistence,
Heart-throb, slow heart-throb, persistent for the next spasm.

I remember, when I was a boy,
I heard the scream of a frog, which was caught with his foot in the
                                        mouth of an up-starting snake;
I remember when I first heard bull-frogs break into sound in the
                                        spring;
I remember hearing a wild goose out of the throat of night
Cry loudly, beyond the lake of waters;
I remember the first time, out of a bush in the darkness, a nightingale's
        piercing cries and gurgles startled the depths of my soul;
I remember the scream of a rabbit as I went through a wood at
                                        midnight;
I remember the heifer in her heat, blorting and blorting through the
        hours, persistent and irrepressible;
I remember my first terror hearing the howl of weird, amorous cats;
I remember the scream of a terrified, injured horse, the sheet-lightning,
And running away from the sound of a woman in labour, something
                                        like an owl whooing,
And listening inwardly to the first bleat of a lamb,
The first wail of an infant,
And my mother singing to herself,
And the first tenor singing of the passionate throat of a young collier,
        who has long since drunk himself to death,

120

The first elements of foreign speech
On wild dark lips.

And more than all these,
And less than all these,
This last,
Strange, faint coition yell
Of the male tortoise at extremity,
Tiny from under the very edge of the farthest far-off horizon of life.

The cross,
The wheel on which our silence first is broken,
Sex, which breaks up our integrity, our single inviolability,
                    our deep silence,
Tearing a cry from us.

Sex, which breaks us into voice, sets us calling across the deeps,
          calling, calling for the complement,
Singing, and calling, and singing again, being answered, having found.

Torn, to become whole again, after long seeking for what is lost,
The same cry from the tortoise as from Christ, the Osiris-cry of
                    abandonment.
That which is whole, torn asunder,
That which is in part, finding its whole again throughout the universe.

                                        D.H. Lawrence

   I mentioned at the beginning of the chapter that the American
poet Ferlinghetti said that the poet is the super-realist. It seems to
me that tackling poetry is vital to the actor because through it he learns
to connect heightened or stylised language (sophisticated language of
any sort including slang and 'in' phrases) with its physical root. The
first thing a baby does is scream, primarily to get air, and then in
order to communicate his needs. The function of speech is to
communicate needs. If you are talking trivialities it is not the
triviality that is important — it is the need to speak it that matters.
Therefore, however stylised or heightened the language is in the
text you are speaking, or however ordinary for that matter,
when you speak it you must root it in the need to speak it, and
speak it in that particular fashion and in those particular words.
   On the practical side, you also get a greater sensitivity and awareness of words from speaking poetry. You become aware of the
physical weight and texture of words, and most importantly, you
become more able to handle them. You become quicker at

perceiving the image and making it precise and, therefore, more confident. Providing that the requirements of poetry are observed, and its contents are listened for, everyone can speak it, as everyone will have a separate perception of it, and this is what makes poetry alive. That is why you can never give anyone an inflection because you will destroy what is particular between that person and the text. You can only urge them to listen to what the text requires and make suggestions. Within the requirements the possibilities are limitless.

6 Listening

Listening accurately is one of the most important factors in using the voice fully, for the accuracy with which we listen relates directly to how we respond vocally. It is something which we tend to take for granted because it is such a basic simple thing.

People tend to listen much less accurately in daily life than they would care to admit. As you listen you are preparing for what you are going to say or do after you have finished listening. The mind is split and is coming to conclusions before it has fully heard. An over-simplified example of this is when you are being introduced to several people, or when you are being given directions of how to get somewhere. Frequently you forget the names or directions very quickly, not because they are more than you can remember, but because the mind is racing ahead to what you are going to say or do after you have finished listening. This is a crude example which is obviously complicated by each individual situation, for the situations themselves will be loaded with other considerations.

This, in another form, is true of the actor. When rehearsing a piece of text, either by himself or in actual rehearsal circumstances, he too often is forming conclusions of what the text should sound like or what he should be presenting before he has discovered what he is actually saying and what the text can say. This of course is part of the actor's situation, the pressure that comes from being judged and the anxiety to present a finished product. But, unless he allows himself time to listen for the possibilities within himself and the text, and unless he allows time for those possibilities to affect him, the vocal result will always be predictable. In his relationship with the other characters he must give himself up wholly to listening so that what they say can affect him. It is only by being this open that the voice will respond freshly and that it will be surprising. It can then take the actor himself by surprise.

When you have passed the rehearsal stage and go into performance the situation is, of course, different. You know the course of the scenes, your relationships, your motives, and you know what you as a character need to say — that is your discipline. But the listening is still important, for the excitement lies in the fact that you are hearing it at that moment and that moment is different from any other moment. Your response is, therefore, for that moment only. If you have the confidence and energy to allow this to happen then the voice will be surprising. This, of course, is why you need the voice free through the practice you do, so that it is able to respond with this degree of awareness.

Is it feasible to do this when it would seem to take a long time to work this way? Ultimately it does not take longer. With breathing, when you become accustomed to taking the breath right down inside you the rhythm of breathing is just as quick. Similarly with listening and receiving: it is getting used to the whole rhythm of work that is important and just thinking about it in these terms is a great part of the battle. Of course, it is the rehearsal situation that makes it difficult to take time; it requires a kind of pressure to do so and a certain resistance from other individuals. It is interesting to notice that the act of listening very often sets up the same sort of tension in the back of the neck and head as happens when you are speaking. This tension affects the freedom with which you can think and, therefore, respond. It is also interesting to notice just what tensions happen in the neck when in fact all you are doing is listening. Once you are aware of it you can use the increased facility you have in relaxation.

Practically, you can familiarise yourself with this whole rhythm of work by using any of the material I have included in this book or any of your own choosing. Take time to read it aloud, not coming to any conclusions but listening for what the words and rhythms contain. Initially you will find every word has significance but gradually, as you become familiar with the text, the image and the particularness of the writing, the words will take their own value in relation to each other. The weight on the individual words will vary enormously, the unweighted words being important in that they lead you on to the weighted ones, and the rhythm of the whole will begin to emerge. It is this relative value of words that you must notice. Take in one thought, speak it, and allow it to lead you to the next.

The Chorus to Act IV of *Henry V*, which I included for work on breathing, is a marvellous passage to see just how this can work. If you examine the first sixteen lines, for example, you will find that the description is so spare that every word matters. For instance, the very first word catches with its immediacy, and each image has to be palpably seen or heard and experienced so that it is real to you. In other words, you have to get in a frame of mind which can accept the terms of the description of the world as a wide vessel. As you become familiar with the detail you can allow the rhythm to take you because, as in everyday speech, you understand through the rhythm as well as through the individual word. You can hear that the suspensions at the end of the lines are an essential part of the meaning, as is the punctuation which gives you the different lengths of phrases and so the different movement. You hear how some phrases are fuller than others and how the rhythm is gathered for a moment on certain words to allow the image to impinge. If you listen for

124

what the words and the rhythm tell you it is extraordinary what
vitality it awakens in you. No word should be taken for granted yet
the overall rhythm into which they fit needs its freedom. You can do
the same with the rest of the passage where it goes into details of
the mood of both the French and the English camps. But it is the
beginning passage which is particularly interesting.

I suggest three passages, two of which I include here, to help you
to go further with this kind of exploration. One is Part 3 of
East Coker, from the *Four Quartets* of T.S. Eliot; this and the
Hopkins poem both have tremendous possibilities for neither make
any statements — their purpose is to discover. If you become
emphatic or present a conclusion with either of them you will cut
out their reverberations. If you receive the words and allow them
to 'touch down', they will take on a meaning which is particular to
you. The passage from *East Coker* is about our fear of death and
the unknown and our search for wholeness, the moment of reality
and of being. Eliot juggles us from one level of consciousness to
another, from one kind of language to another — from Samson's
first cry at his blindness into very informal everyday language, and
then to the mystical utterance of the end. It is a continual
discovery of feelings which are not quite tangible but which are part
of a primitive consciousness. The Hopkins poem is also about
death. It describes growing old and the loss of innocence and therefore beauty; but in the end you are brought to hope through his
own religious belief. The music comes from the way he uses the
words and not out of an idea of a cadence. The words answer and
echo each other in a curious way yet always taking on the sense.
Eliot makes you sensitive to the precise weight and measurement
words have: Hopkins charges the ear with sound and makes you open
to an area where the sound influences and changes the sense. The
extract from Shaw's *Man and Superman* is totally different. It is
didactic and full of ideas but he puts over his ideas through enquiry.
The listener has to be open to that enquiry and he can only be so if
he allows the ideas to be fully realised.

THE LEADEN ECHO AND THE GOLDEN ECHO

(Maidens' song from St. Winefred's Well)

THE LEADEN ECHO

How to keép — is there ány any, is there none such, nowhere
    known some, bow or brooch to braid or brace, láce,
    latch or catch or key to keep
Back beauty, keep it, beauty, beauty, beauty . . . from vanishing
                           away?
Ó is thre no frowning of these wrinkles, rankèd wrinkles deep,
Dówn? no waving off of these most mournful messengers,
    still messengers, sad and stealing messengers of grey? —
No there's none, there's none, O no there's none,
Nor can you long be, what you now are, called fair,
Do what you may do, what, do what you may,
And wisdom is early to despair:
Be beginning; since, no, nothing can be done
To keep at bay
Age and age's evils, hoar hair,
Ruck and wrinkle, drooping, dying, death's worst, winding
    sheets, tombs and worms and tumbling to decay;
So be beginning, be beginning to despair.
O there's none: no no no there's none:
Be beginning to despair, to despair,
Despair, despair, despair, despair.

THE GOLDEN ECHO

                            Spare!
There is one, yes I have one (Hush there!)
Only not within seeing of the sun,
Not within the singeing of the strong sun,
Tall sun's tingeing, or treacherous the tainting of the earth's air,
Somewhere elsewhere there is ah well where! one,
One. Yes I cán tell such a key, I dó know such a place,
Where whatever's prizèd and passes of us, everything that's fresh
    and fast flying of us, seems to us sweet of us and swiftly
    away with, done away with, undone,
Undone, done with, soon done with, and yet dearly and
                        dangerously sweet
Of us, the wimpled-water-dimpled, not-by-morning-matchèd face,
The flower of beauty, fleece of beauty, too too apt to, ah!
                    to fleet,
Never fleets more, fastened with the tenderest truth
To its own best being and its loveliness of youth: it is an

everlastingness of, O it is an all youth!
Come then, your ways and airs and looks, locks, maidengear,
    gallantry and gaiety and grace,
Winning ways, airs innocent, maiden manners, sweet looks, loose
    locks, long locks, lovelocks, gaygear, going gallant,
                 girlgrace —
Resign them, sign them, seal them, send them, motion them
              with breath,
And with sighs soaring, soaring síghs, deliver
Them; beauty-in-the-ghost, deliver it, early now, long before death
Give beauty back, beauty, beauty, beauty, back to God,
    beauty's self and beauty's giver.
See; not a hair is, not an eyelash, not the least lash lost; every
    hair
Is, hair of the head, numbered.
Nay, what we had lighthanded left in surly the mere mould
Will have waked and have waxed and have walked with the wind
    what while we slept,
This side, that side hurling a heavyheaded hundredfold
What while we, while we slumbered.
O then, weary then whý should we tread? O why are we so
    haggard at the heart, so care-coiled, care-killed, so fagged,
    so fashed, so cogged, so cumbered,
When the thing we freely fórfeit is kept with fonder a care,
Fonder a care kept than we could have kept it, kept
Far with fonder a care (and we, we should have lost it) finer,
    fonder
A care kept. — Where kept? Do but tell us where kept, where. —
Yonder. — What high as that! We follow, now we follow. —
    Yonder, yes yonder, yonder,
Yonder.

                          Gerard Manley Hopkins

From *MAN AND SUPERMAN*

The Devil: And is Man any the less destroying himself for all this boasted brain of his? Have you walked up and down upon the earth lately? I have; and I have examined Man's wonderful inventions. And I tell you that in the arts of life man invents nothing; but in the arts of death he outdoes Nature herself, and produces by chemistry and machinery all the slaughter of plague, pestilence, and famine. The peasant I tempt today eats and drinks what was eaten and drunk by the peasants of ten thousand years ago; and the house he lives in has not altered as much in a thousand centuries as the fashion of a lady's bonnet in a score of weeks. But when he goes out to slay, he carries a marvel of mechanism that lets loose at the touch of his finger all the hidden molecular energies, and leaves the javelin, the arrow, the blowpipe of his fathers far behind. In the arts of peace Man is a bungler. I have seen his cotton factories and the like, with machinery that a greedy dog could have invented if it had wanted money instead of food. I know his clumsy typewriters and bungling locomotives and tedious bicycles: they are toys compared to the Maxim gun, the submarine torpedo boat. There is nothing in Man's industrial machinery but his greed and sloth: his heart is in his weapons. This marvellous force of Life of which you boast is a force of Death: Man measures his strength by his destructiveness. What is his religion? An excuse for hating me. What is his law? An excuse for hanging you. What is his morality? Gentility! An excuse for consuming without producing. What is his art? An excuse for gloating over pictures of slaughter. What are his politics? Either the worship of a despot because a despot can kill, or parliamentary cock-fighting. I spent an evening lately in a certain celebrated legislature, and heard the pot lecturing the kettle for its blackness, and ministers answering questions. When I left I chalked up on the door the old nursery saying 'Ask no questions and you will be told no lies.' I bought a sixpenny family magazine, and found it full of pictures of young men shooting and stabbing one another. I saw a man die: he was a London bricklayer's labourer with seven children. He left seventeen pounds club money; and his wife spent it all on his funeral and went into the workhouse with the children next day. She would not have spent sevenpence on her children's schooling: the law had to force her to let them be taught gratuitously; but on death she spent all she had. Their imagination glows, their energies rise up at the idea of death, these people: they love it; and the more horrible it is the more they enjoy it. Hell is a place far above their comprehension: they derive their notion of it from two of the greatest fools that ever lived, an Italian and an Englishman. The

Italian described it as a place of mud, frost, filth, fire, and venomous serpents: all torture. This ass, when he was not lying about me, was maundering about some woman whom he saw once in the street. The Englishman described me as being expelled from heaven by cannons and gunpowder; and to this day every Briton believes that the whole of his silly story is in the Bible. What else he says I do not know; for it is all in a long poem which neither I nor anyone else ever succeeded in wading through. It is the same in everything. The highest form of literature is the tragedy, a play in which everybody is murdered at the end. In the old chronicles you read of earthquakes and pestilences, and are told that these shewed the power and majesty of God and the littleness of Man. Nowadays the chronicles describe battles. In a battle two bodies of men shoot at one another with bullets and explosive shells until one body runs away, when the others chase the fugitives on horseback and cut them to pieces as they fly. And this, the chronicle concludes, shews the greatness and majesty of empires, and the littleness of the vanquished. Over such battles the people run about the streets yelling with delight, and egg their Governments on to spend hundreds of millions of money in the slaughter, whilst the strongest Ministers dare not spend an extra penny in the pound against the poverty and pestilence through which they themselves daily walk. I could give you a thousand instances; but they all come to the same thing: the power that governs the earth is not the power of Life but of Death; and the inner need that has nerved Life to the effort of organizing itself into the human being is not the need for higher life but for a more efficient engine of destruction. The plague, the famine, the earthquake, the tempest were too spasmodic in their action; the tiger and crocodile were too easily satiated and not cruel enough; something more constantly, more ruthlessly, more ingeniously destructive was needed; and that something was Man, the inventor of the rack, the stake, the gallows, the electric chair; of sword and gun and poison gas: above all, of justice, duty, patriotism, and all the other isms by which even those who are clever enough to be humanely disposed are persuaded to become the most destructive of all the destroyers.

G.B. Shaw

7 Using the Voice

You have found how to prepare the voice to the standard of development which you have attained at the moment. You must now look at the specific problems which will come in work.

You have already seen that one of the main problems is size: the size of place which you have to fill, the emotional size of the character, and, sometimes, the actor's own size.

I shall deal firstly with filling space. This has much to do with your own gauging of an auditorium which can only come with experience. Acoustically, it is useful to think of the auditorium floor as a sounding board. If you have a particularly difficult area to fill, one which is acoustically dead, you will find that if you aim vocally at a point along the floor half to two-thirds of the way back the sound will spring off the floor and fill the space easily. Whereas, if you just aim the sound up and out the clarity will go and the space will not be filled. It is useful to do the humming exercises focusing at different points in the auditorium and finding the point at which the voice carries best. The more you can experiment with large spaces the more sensitive you will become to the problem. When you have found the most satisfactory focal point speak some text, first focusing it and then speaking it up and out — notice the difference. Then try speaking the text concentrating on the focal point in your mind; but move about and turn away, keeping the sound focused. This is an excellent exercise for helping you to come to terms with the exterior conditions. The vocal filling of space is to do with sharpness of diction and the precise placing of word and tone. It is also connected with timing — you need fractionally longer and more fricative consonants for the words to reach and you have to allow for the time the voice takes to reach to the back of a large space: the sound has to follow through. It is also affected by your own reaching out and sense of sharing — that is, being on terms with your audience and, within the context of the character and play, not hiding but sharing. It is incredible what a difference this makes to the voice. An actor may have great concentration and be doing interesting work but, unless the audience is included in the concentration it is not drawn to listen. If the actor can look at his audience within his point of reference then the voice becomes alive. It is as simple as this: if the eyes are not communicating the voice will not be communicating completely either.

The physical size of the actor himself, particularly a male actor, very often dictates how he uses his voice. If an actor is small there is frequently a compulsion to compensate and, therefore, to force the voice down to get a false kind of resonance instead of finding the resonance within himself. This, contrary to what the actor may feel, is limiting for it makes the listener aware of the actor's excuse for himself; it also irons out much of the interesting flexibility in the voice. If an actor is particularly large it is interesting to notice that the voice, though resonant, often has a soft quality and lacks real definition and energy. This again is compensation for size or perhaps fear of the power which is there. The voice must be relative to the person.

The second problem which can arise is that of emotional size of a part. When working on a character of classical stature or one which has great emotional size the actor will always feel pressure because he feels that he may not be able to fill out this size. The temptation here is to resolve the problem by extra volume. If you do this you inevitably lose the specific reasoning and conceptions of the character which are its size. The size must be found through coming to terms with the particular ideas and feelings of the character and, therefore, with the words that are used. If you are working on a part like this it is essential that you talk it through very quietly, for it is only by doing this that you will continue to open out the richness of the character. The strength will come from your own vocal firmness and weight which you have already found. It is an extraordinary thing that when you use volume without great sensitivity you not only iron out the subtlety and manoeuvrability of your own voice but you actually create certain mental tensions so that you cease to think specifically. Volume has little to do with either filling space or size of character though, of course, some parts need more sustained sound than others and therefore require more preparation. There are times when an outburst of volume or an extra cry or shout is needed, but it must be used sparingly or it ceases to be remarkable; it must only be released when it can no longer be contained. The listener cannot take too much volume as it will eventually lose its impact. When you do increase the volume it must always be matched by an increase in the weight of the consonant: the more volume you use the more consonant value you need to break the sound up into words. The increase in energy needed for extra volume must always be found on the breath and never by forcing energy from the throat.

In order to find volume without tension, whether it is for sustained intensity or for short bursts, take some part of the text and do it lying on the floor. Take time to find your relaxation and to get the breathing working properly and then start the text. Say it very quietly at first, making sure that it is firmly rooted to the breath; gradually increase the volume, taking care not to pitch it up but keeping the same flexibility of inflection as when you are thinking it through so that the sense remains clear. Increase the volume gradually in this way, watching closely that you do not become tense and that the sound does not go into the throat. The moment you start to get tense or find that you move any part of yourself as if beating the voice out physically, stop, release the tensions, and then continue. I do not mean that you must not move when speaking: it is simply that you need to be able to convey all the strength in the voice without movement so that you will then be free to choose what movement you want to make. You must be able to differentiate between your own personal tension and the tension of the character. When you can convey everything through freedom then you can move or remain still as you wish. If you cannot speak the text without becoming tense yourself or without certain involuntary movements then you limit yourself to your own tension.

It is interesting to notice that, when you force yourself to be strong instead of reaching down for your own strength, you also force the voice into the throat because there you feel control. But by being so much in control you reduce your power because you do not allow yourself to receive energy from the text. You, therefore, reduce the text to your size instead of expanding to its size. Many actors have this problem of not being able to let go in the back of the neck: they are, in some way, monitoring themselves and dare not let go for fear of losing that particular control. This will, however, always limit the voice.

In order to acquire strength you must do a great deal of work on relaxation and using the breath. There comes a time when, providing you are quite free and there is no tension in the neck, it is helpful to shout parts of the text, perhaps moving about, just to find freedom. It is always good to vary the approach to work otherwise you get stuck in a particular way of doing things. It is a delicate business and you must use your intuition to discover what will help you at a particular moment. If you are trying for strength in a part it is very important to concentrate on where you key the voice. One tends to keep the pitch down and so limit the range which is, of course, dull. Keying the voice on a low note should not rule out the high notes for, in fact, you need them in contrast to sound off the low notes, and it certainly will not lighten the effect of the voice.

When exploring character in the voice the same criterion applies. The vocal transformation of yourself into another character must come from the words and rhythm of the writing; if this leads you into a different way of speaking that is fine, provided no tension comes from it. The words and thought must lead you to a way of speaking and if you start by thinking of finding a different voice or of putting on some sort of sound which is a distortion of your own voice, it will limit you and be a strain, and most probably will lack simplicity. If you require a range which is a little out of your normal middle range work at it slowly, using the breathing and singing exercises already given, and you will gradually extend the voice to the point required. You cannot allow tension to come into the voice under any circumstances for over a period of time it will lead to strain and the voice will suffer physically.

It is often the case that, because of lack of trust and misplacement of energy, and because it is difficult to extract and separate personal tension from the tensions of the part, an actor fogs his communication by signalling. This seems to be one of the greatest and most frequent traps into which an actor falls. I mean by that that when an actor feels he does not just feel – he signals that he is feeling. He does not simply understand but signals his appreciation. When he is romantic a romantic vocal quality underlines what is already in the words and the action. When he is suffering a suffering quality appears which does not illumine anything for the audience and is usually monotonous. An actor who needs to be active and virile pushes at the audience and blasts them with noise and energy which usually comes from the throat. As soon as the listener feels these things being pushed at him he steps back, because exhibited reaction makes people recoil. As I said earlier, in real life when someone is over-anxious to tell you something you are irritated and want to get away.

If this signalling is happening (and here you have to depend on and be open to criticism) you must be quite sure of the reason why it is happening. Is it a lack of trust which makes you push and underline what is already in the script or is it a wrong kind of showmanship which makes you display what the audience does not really want to see – that is, the effect of the feelings on you instead of the reason for those feelings? It is important to find out so that you can make the right kind of adjustment.

In other words, if you have a part which has emotional size and involves anger, authority and so on, and you shout, producing over-balance of sound to word, the audience will not listen and will not know the reason for the power. You must find the strength within yourself, and sit on your own weight and power, releasing the right vocal energy. This, coupled with the energy from the text, will have size and the audience will be involved with the reason for that size. If you have a part which is witty and extravagant you will not make it funny by meddling with the inflections – that is, by telling the audience that it is funny. The humour will come if you have found the necessity for those words. Similarly, if you have a part with great depth of feeling and the voice becomes romantic, what you are doing is telling the audience that you can feel but you do not convince them of the reason for that feeling: they do not, therefore, totally believe it.

133

Let me give you some examples of this. In the lovers' scenes in
A Midsummer Night's Dream the lovers are romantic, youthful and
full of ardour, but if the characters are played with a romantic
quality in the voice the scenes will become repetitive and boring. But
if you realise that the romance and youth and ardour is in the very
argument of the text the scenes will have their own energy and drive.
It is the same with any romantic text: the excitement lies in the
discovery of the feeling, which can be done through finding the
precise meaning of the words. This does not mean that the text should
be made to sound ordinary or everyday because the words are not
ordinary nor is the situation. The marvellous thing about Peter
Brook's production of *The Dream* was the way that everything came
out of the text. The physical life that the actors had on the stage was
the result of the total communication between themselves. I worked
on the voices during the rehearsal period and it was fascinating to see
how, working in small groups on other poetic texts besides
Shakespeare, aiming solely to communicate text as directly as possible,
their communication with each other was reinforced on the stage.
The problem which the actors had in the small groups, that of being
absolutely specific with the voice and with the words, was invariably
the same problem they had in acting.

Another example of quite different writing and substance is
Webster's *Duchess of Malfi*, the story being more fantastic and violent
than is within the real experience of probably anyone acting in it. If
you force its brutality and violence you will miss, because it will then
be loud and mean nothing. You must receive those images and words
with their incredible mixture of elegance and decadence, the physical
presence they have of themselves, and their palpable form, and allow
the audience to receive them with total directness; they will then
understand that world. The play is full of the most remarkable
imagery of violence, disease, decay, bestiality, and geometrical
precision. In metaphysical writing the sense of mortality is always
present. Ferdinand talks about the Duchess's court thus:

> You live in a rank pasture here, i'th'court,
> There is a kind of honey-dew that's deadly:
> 'Twill poison your fame; look to't; be not cunning:
> For they whose faces do belie their hearts
> Are witches, ere they arrive at twenty years,
> Ay: and give the devil suck.

When Ferdinand hears of her secret marriage, you recognize the
beginning of his madness in the extraordinary nature of the image:

> I have this night digg'd up a mandrake.

Bosola speaks about his and the human condition:

> . . . . Observe my meditation now:
> What thing is in this outward form of man
> To be belov'd? We account it ominous,
> If nature do produce a colt, or lamb,
> A fawn, or goat, in any limb resembling
> A man; and fly from't as a prodigy.
> Man stands amaz'd to see his deformity,
> In any other creature but himself.
> But in our own flesh, though we bear diseases
> Which have their true names only ta'en from beasts,
> As the most ulcerous wolf, and swinish measle;
> Though we are eaten up of lice, and worms,
> And though continually we bear about us
> A rotten and dead body, we delight
> To hide it in rich tissue: all our fear
> Nay, all our terror, is lest our physician
> Should put us in the ground, to be made sweet.

In coping with a text like this you have to find the reason of the
speech — that is, you have to make the top logical sense clear and
pursue the thought. You must weave your way through the
extravagance of its utterance, which involves experiencing the weight
and form of those particular images so that the audience can realise
them fully. You also have to root all this down to the particular
emotional need of the character which is contained in those precise
words, their sound containing some of their meaning.

If you are dealing with a comedy like *The Importance of Being
Earnest* the humour is in the total belief of those characters in what
they are saying. If the actor tinges this with the smallest awareness of
his understanding of its extravagance and why it is funny, or makes
any comment at all, it will not work. He must come down to the
simplicity and logic of those words.

The same is true of a modern text. The words used may be those
of absolutely ordinary, everyday speech, but the situation is special
and those words and that rhythm are special to that character. In
Beckett or Pinter, for instance, the way the words are strung together
contains their own particular desolation. In Osborne's invective the
viciousness comes out of the need to choose those particular words.
Tennessee Williams has a particular music which, in its decadence and
corruption, reminds you of Webster. One could go on endlessly
giving examples of the tremendous flexibility of language because
each text you tackle adds to that experience; the point that matters
is that there is so much to be found in the text you use. American

Method acting had a tremendous influence on the use of the voice. It puts the emphasis on the physical involvement of the character, very often to the exclusion of the word and to the point of being almost inarticulate. It was probably a necessary move at the time and very salutary, for the actor's style had, in general, become too dependent on the voice and therefore sterile. But I think that people were led to believe that this particular style of acting was more exciting than it actually was; for any imbalance either way cannot be totally true, and using the voice is just as physical as using any other part of the body. If the voice is used to the exclusion of the physical need it will not be wholly convincing or wholly informed; and if the physical involvement becomes more important than the word it will reduce the character and will eventually become tedious. This may sound pompous, but 'Suit the action to the word, the word to the action, with this special observance, that you o'erstep not the modesty of nature,' must surely be the ultimate in advice.

The actor, of course, has to deal with a lot of very ordinary text which is sometimes not well-written and quite often just bad. This often tends to make him by-pass the word on purpose and go for the motive and action through the scene. It is extraordinary how, by working on good text for yourself, you will be enabled to deal with the not so good.

To sum up: you have to prepare the voice as well as possible and make it as skilled as you can. You have to stretch it so that it can compass and respond to whatever text you have and so that it can be surprising. You must get rid of all the rubbish! By that I mean that you have constantly to pare away all unnecessary colouring and tension and the paraphernalia which you feel you need to convince an audience and which, in fact, gets in the way of direct communication. I am sure that one of the actor's greatest concerns is the fear of not feeling enough and, therefore, of not being interesting enough. The greater the emotion in the part the more he tries to convince the audience of his feeling and so ceases to be specific. You know that this often occurs but it is difficult to trust yourself. You must believe that you have a right to be there.

Summary of Exercises

I include here a summary of the exercises to serve as a reminder of the areas to be worked on. Put in this concise form, this will perhaps make you particularly aware of the discipline needed.

These exercises are for greater freedom in the voice, and to make one increasingly aware of the difference between one's personal tension and the tension of the character and situation. Unnecessary tension is energy wasted. It is important to clarify and inform the word, because it is the word that is the result of all you think and feel and which finally impinges on the audience. The word must be crystal-clear and not over-balanced by tone, though the more whole the sound the more conviction it carries, and the more satisfactory it is to the ear. This balance is vital.

Ultimately, what makes the voice particular is the mental-physical tie-up. The voice must be free and responsive enough to reflect what you think and feel. It must be as interesting as what you have to communicate. It should always be able to surprise. Its job is to make the listener remark what is remarkable.

RELAXATION AND BREATHING

1 Lie on the floor, feeling the back as spread as possible, i.e. the shoulders and back widening and the head lengthening out of the back. Do not get a feeling of sinking into the floor but rather of spreading over it.

   Feel the shoulders, neck and arms free so the joints are easing away from each other and not pressed in.

2 Put your hands on the side of the ribs, where the rib cage is widest and:
a Breathe in then sigh out pushing all the air right out; wait until you feel the muscles between the ribs needing to move, then fill slowly in again feeling the ribs widening at the back and sides. Try not to lift the top of the chest. Repeat several times.
b Breathe in, then out slowly for 10 counts, being aware of the muscles between the ribs controlling the breath. Increase the count out to 15 and then to 20.
c Breathe in all the way round. Put one hand on your diaphragm and sigh out from there several times, gently but firmly, to feel where the breath comes from. Then put a little sound to it on 'ER', touching it off like a drum. Then a more sustained sound on 'AH', 'AY' and 'I', joining the breath to the sound.

d Breathe in so that the ribs are open. Put one hand on the diaphragm and sigh out easily through an open throat. Then fill in again and count to 6 aloud on that breath. Continue with a short piece of text you know, making sure you fill right down each time you breathe so that the breath starts the sound. Root the sound to the breath.

Keep checking that the shoulders and neck are free.

3 Get into a good position, either sitting or standing with the back widening and lengthening.

Head
Drop forward and lift slowly, feeling the muscles in the back of the neck pulling up.
Drop back and lift.
Drop to the sides and stretch and lift.
Roll round as fully as possible.
Tense slightly back — relax and feel the difference.
Nod gently from an upright position, feeling the muscles in the back of the neck free.
A very small roll round to get the sensation of freedom of movement. The head may be still but not fixed.

Shoulders
Lift and drop gently, noticing what it feels like when they are dropped.

4 a With your hands behind your head — as relaxed as possible, breathe in and sigh right out — the last little bit. Wait until the ribs need to move, then let the ribs widen and fill in. Repeat two or three times only. This opens the chest.
  b Hands down or on the side of your ribs. Breathe in fully and out slowly for 10, 15 and 20 counts, being aware of the muscles between the ribs controlling the breath.
  c Breathe in and sigh out from the diaphragm on 'ER' feeling the breath and the sound together. Then on a more sustained vowel 'AH' and 'I'. When you feel the sound is rooted down speak some text on that breath.

Always keep the upper chest, neck and shoulders free.

When speaking your text reach down to the diaphragm for the sound so that you get a sense of the tone coming unhindered from there. The chest can then contribute to the resonance. The throat should feel entirely free. The important thing is to feel the muscles working, i.e., the muscles between the ribs and the diaphragm, because it is the muscular tone that gives the vocal tone substance. Of course, you exaggerate the movement of the muscles in exercise simply to be aware of them. Ultimately, the breathing should be economical and smooth, but the extra energy needed to project, so that you can keep the intimacy and subtlety and yet be large enough, should come from this whole use of the voice.

MUSCULARITY

1 Insert the bone-prop and exercise the tongue and lip muscles:

Tongue-tip

a
la	la	la	la
lala	lala	lala	lala
lalala	lalala	lalala	lalala

Make the tongue drop to the bottom each time.

b
tetete	tetete	tetete	tah
dedede	dedede	dedede	dah
nenene	nenene	nenene	nah

Back of tongue

c
kekeke	kekeke	kekeke	kah
gegege	gegege	gegege	gah
	kekeke	tetete	
	gegege	dedede	

Lips

d
pepepe	pepepe	pepepe	pah
bebebe	bebebe	bebebe	bah
mememe	mememe	mememe	mah
mememe	nenene	— keep this clear of the nose.	

In exercise, press the tongue and lip muscles hard so you become aware of them. They also contribute to the resonance and give it dimension.

e
AH	OO		
AH	AW	OO	
AH	AW	OO	OW
MAH	MAW	MOO	MOW
PAH	PAW	POO	POW
BAH	BAW	BOO	BOW

Front of the tongue

Keep the back of the tongue relaxed.

f	AH	EE		
	AH	AY	EE	
	AH	AY	EE	I
	LAH	LAY	LEE	LI
	TAH	TAY	TEE	TI
	DAH	DAY	DEE	DI
	NAH	NAY	NEE	NI

Feel the front of the tongue arching upwards.

g	EAR	AIR
	LEAR	LAIR
	TEAR	TAIR
	DEAR	DAIR
	NEAR	NAIR

Feel the tongue moving down.

h Without the prop say: Vvvvvvvvvv' and Zzzzzzzzzz' several times, feeling the vibration on the lips and tongue.

In all these exercises rapidity is not important. It is the firmness of the muscular movement which is essential and the awareness of the vibration on the consonant, because the tone must come from where the words are formed. It is this muscular firmness which makes the words carry and which is the physical part of projection. The voice should come unhindered from the diaphragm to be formed into words and 'sent-off' by the lips and tongue. It should then be effortless and have no strain on the throat.

2 To open the throat, without the prop:

a Drop the jaw and feel the tongue and neck quite relaxed and open. Make the muscles in the back of the tongue and palate work by saying 'gegege' very hard, pushing the tongue up to the back of the palate and feeling it tensed. Then drop the tongue and feel it relaxed, so you are aware of both the tension and the relaxation.

b Repeat in this way:

gegege — with the palate and the tongue tensed at the back.
gegege — with the palate and tongue dropped.

Hear the difference in sound:

gegege — tense
gegege — relaxed
AH   — dropped and open

Then with relaxed tongue and palate:

gegege — AH
gegege — AY
gegege — I

Keep the consonants firm and the vowels open.

c Then, using plenty of breath sing out on 'AY' and 'I', making sure the sound is starting at the diaphragm.

Repeat this, swinging down from side to side with your arms and head, making sure the head drops completely each time.

3 Stand normally and work on a piece of text, combining the result of all the exercises, i.e., breathing, relaxation, and muscularity.